Peter Hepplewhite is an escaped history teacher, currently hiding in the cellars of Tyne and Wear Archive Service where he works as Education Officer. He has been a freelance writer for more than ten years, starting with school textbooks (Boo!) before he realized that wild animals were more fun.

Mike Phillips spends each day illustrating books from a shed at the bottom of his garden, in Essex. He likes nothing better than to get his teeth into a juicy book of animal stories.

Also available from Macmillan

Amazing Animals: Animals to the Rescue
Peter Hepplewhite and Neil Tonge

Amazing Animals: Animals in Danger
Peter Hepplewhite and Neil Tonge

Maneaters

Peter Hepplewhite

Illustrated by Mike Phillips

MACMILLAN CHILDREN'S BOOKS

First published 2001
by Macmillan Children's Books
a division of Macmillan Publishers Ltd
25 Eccleston Place, London SW1W 9NF
Basingstoke and Oxford
www.panmacmillan.com

Associated companies throughout the world

ISBN 0 330 48357 9

1 3 5 7 9 8 6 4 2

A CIP catalogue record for this book is available from the British Library.

Printed by Mackays of Chatham plc, Chatham, Kent.

Contents

Introduction

Maneaters! The word conjures up images of sleek animal killers with cruel teeth and raking claws. The thought of ever coming face-to-face with a shark, lion or tiger sends shivers down our spines. They are untamed nature at its worst – beasts that can compete with humans and even prey on them. We live in a world where some children have to go on farm visits to meet pigs, sheep and cows. Is it any wonder that wolves and crocodiles seem strange, threatening and exotic? In the popular imagination, predators have become monsters. Hollywood films like *Jaws* credit them with supernatural strength and evil intelligence whilst real-life animal attacks are guaranteed to grab the headlines. But how true is this picture? Who should be afraid of who?

A shepherd spits in disgust. 'What good is a wolf?' he asks. 'You can't eat him and you can't milk him.' Sadly he speaks for many people who can see little value in animals that cannot pay their way. Across the planet the wilderness is in retreat as the human population soars. Predators are killed out of fear, poached for their

skins or body parts or driven to the edge of extinction as their habitat is destroyed.

This book brings you chilling animal attack stories from around the world and amazing facts about some of the mightiest predators. But it also brings you some issues surrounding their fate. The future of a growing number of the world's species depends upon the way people think about them – even the deadliest predators. Are we prepared to share our planet with these wild animals or are their days numbered? The decisions will be made in your lifetime. There are no easy answers.

Sharks

Your happy holiday flight to Florida has ditched in the sea. You grab your life-jacket and escape the sinking plane. While you float in the warm Caribbean waters, waiting for rescue, what thoughts might flicker across your mind – thoughts you had better not mention to Auntie Joan paddling next to you?

Pirates? No

Hurricanes? No

Earthquakes? No

Sharks. Yes!

Shark attack is probably the most feared natural danger known to humans. But are such fears justified? Read on and shiver . . .

Shark Attack Reports

Sailors have always dreaded abandoning ship in tropical seas. True, they can survive for longer in warm waters, but there is danger beneath the waves – sharks!

Attack Report 1: The Luckiest Survivor

A glance at the ragged circle of scars on the body of Rodney Fox is enough to know that he is one of the luckiest men alive. On 8 December 1963, he was taking part in the South Australian State Spear Fishing Championship at Aldinga Beach, just south of Adelaide. He was coming to the end of his first dive and had no idea of the terror that was only seconds away. Suddenly, a great white shark burst out of the gloomy water beneath him and clamped its massive jaws round his torso. Rows of teeth punctured his chest and back.

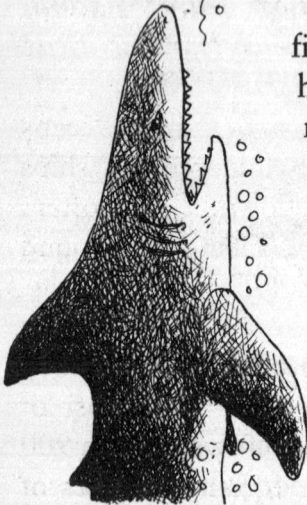

The assault was so quick that at first Rodney felt no pain. As he hurtled through the water in the mouth of the shark, all he was aware of was the terrible crushing pressure. He realized he was about to die! With a courage born of instinct and panic Rodney fought back. He hammered his right fist into the shark's left eye socket, fingers scrabbling to tear out the eyeball. When the beast jerked back and released him, his arm slipped into its mouth and was ripped to the bone by razor-sharp teeth.

Now the shark had tasted blood it was not about to let him escape. It lunged at Rodney again but this time missed his flesh and seized the fishing float fastened to his diving belt. With this firmly in its maw the great white dived, dragging him down with it. Frantically Rodney tried to unbuckle the belt but his fingers felt numb and useless. Then, incredibly, he was free. The line to the float had snapped, severed by the shark's teeth. Gasping for breath he clawed his way to the surface and was hauled into a nearby boat.

By now Rodney was in a desperate state. That first cruel bite had ripped open his rib cage, upper stomach and lungs. His ribs were crushed and the flesh had been stripped from his left arm. In hospital, surgeons fought for four hours to save his life. He needed 462 stitches to close his wounds.

Attack Report 2: The *Nova Scotia*

During World War II, the Pacific and Indian Oceans became a vast battleground, with hundreds of ships sunk and thousands of planes shot down. All too often, the helpless crews, swimming for their lives, found themselves the targets of these sleek killers.

On 28 November 1942, the Liverpool steamer *Nova Scotia* was 48 kilometres (30 miles) off the coast of Natal, South Africa, bound for Cape Town. Of the 900 or so people on board, 765 were Italian prisoners of war being shipped to work camps. The *Nova Scotia* was close to safety but would never reach it – a German U-boat was waiting. A salvo of torpedoes ripped her apart and she sank within seven minutes. Amazingly, most of the crew and prisoners grabbed life-jackets and escaped unhurt into the sea. Yet the horror had only just begun.

Perhaps it was the scent of blood from the injured, or perhaps it was the noise of 900 men struggling in the water – but soon sharks gathered and began a feeding frenzy. By the time a rescue ship arrived, 60 long hours later, there were only 192 survivors. And even as they were hoisted aboard, the Portuguese crew had to use boat hooks to fight off huge numbers of snapping sharks.

Many of the bodies that were recovered later were found with limbs missing – they had been bitten off. Mercifully, some of the victims may have died of thirst or drowned and then been eaten. However, most of the shipwrecked men were young and fit enough to have survived until help came. Their last hours were spent watching their hunters circling ever closer.

Attack Report 3: The *Indianapolis*

On 26 July 1945, the 13-year-old United States cruiser *Indianapolis* arrived at Tinian in the Marianas Islands, in the West Pacific Ocean. She was carrying a fateful cargo, the detonation device for the first atomic bomb soon to be dropped on the city of Hiroshima. Mission accomplished, she set off to join Task Force 95 and train for the invasion of Japan. But the *Indianapolis* never arrived.

Just before midnight on 29 July, she was intercepted by the Japanese submarine, 1-58. Commander Mochitsura opened fire with six torpedoes and at least two found their target. The torpedoes set off a chain of violent explosions in the fuel and ammunition aboard and blew off the bow of the ship. Only 850 out of a crew of 1,196 made it into the sea alive. Soaked in fuel oil, wracked by thirst and suffering from hypothermia, many died as they floated in their life-jackets. Others were to endure the same ordeal as the men from the *Nova Scotia* – days in the water as shark bait.

By July 1945, the war was almost over and no one missed the *Indianapolis* or suspected that she had come to grief. It was not until 2 August that a navy spotter plane happened to sight the survivors. When the rescue ships arrived there were only 316 men left alive.

Seaman Leo Dane Cox remembered the grisly wait:

You could see down about 20 or 25 feet and see sharks, some 10 feet long, making lazy circles. Then they'd flip up just as fast as you can imagine and grab somebody. Once a shark grabbed one of my buddies just three feet from me. It was pure luck it wasn't me.

Woody Eugene James, another survivor, wrote later:

Day 3
The day wore on and the sharks were around, hundreds of them. You'd hear guys scream, especially late in the afternoon. Seemed like the sharks were

worst late in the afternoon. Then they fed all night too. Everything would be quiet then you'd hear somebody scream and you knew a shark had got him.

The *Indianapolis* set several grim wartime records when she sank:

- The last American warship to be sunk in World War II.
- The last victim of the Imperial Japanese Navy.
- The last ship to be sunk by submarine.
- The worst American naval disaster with a death toll of 883.
- And the worst American shark attack.

The Beach with the Most Shark Attacks

This unenviable reputation belongs to the resort of Amanzimtoti, near Durban, South Africa. But don't cross it off your holiday list, because the risk is tiny – only eleven attacks, two of them fatal, have been recorded between 1940 and 1998.

Over the past 40 years there has been an average of only three or four shark attacks a year in South Africa and less than 10 per cent of these have been fatal. However, in 1998 incidents of reported shark attacks increased. The newspapers were suddenly full of shark scare stories. Two reasons have been put forward to explain this surge in attacks:

I DIDN'T BRING A CAN OPENER, DID YOU?

- *Cage Diving* – This is a growing sport/hobby. Divers are lowered from boats in cages and throw bait into the ocean to attract sharks. Safely behind bars they can eyeball a great white or a tiger shark. But is there a risk? Are sharks learning to link a human activity with food?

- *Food Shortages* – The South African White Shark Research Institute argues that the problem is that over-fishing has wrecked fish stocks. Hungry sharks are coming into coastal waters more often to search for food.

The Kwa-Zulu-Natal Sharks Board in South Africa offers helpful hints for worried beach users:

- Swim at beaches protected by shark nets.
- Avoid swimming with an open wound as sharks can detect blood and other body fluids.
- Don't swim at dawn, dusk and at night when sharks are most active.
- Don't swim alone.
- Be cautious especially when spear fishing. (After Rodney's experience do you need to be told this?)

The Shark Attack Files

The world's best database on shark incidents is the International Shark Attack Files at the Florida Museum of Natural History. Check out their fascinating website at: www.flmnh.ufl. edu/fish/Sharks /ISAF/ISAF.htm

The database began as a research programme for the United States Navy in 1958 and has since gathered information on thousands of attacks on humans from shark hotspots such as Australia and South Africa as well as the USA. If you are unlucky enough to be involved in a head-to-head tussle with a great white, the museum wants to know every detail. As well as the obvious details their questions include:

- What kind of water was the victim in – salt, fresh, brackish, clear, murky, muddy?

- If the victim was in shallow water what was he/she doing – wading, splashing, sitting on the bottom?
- If the victim was fishing what was he/she doing – hooking a fish, netting a fish, spear fishing, holding a fish?
- What did the shark do after the attack – stay fastened to the victim and be forcibly removed (ouch), follow the victim to the shore, leave the area?

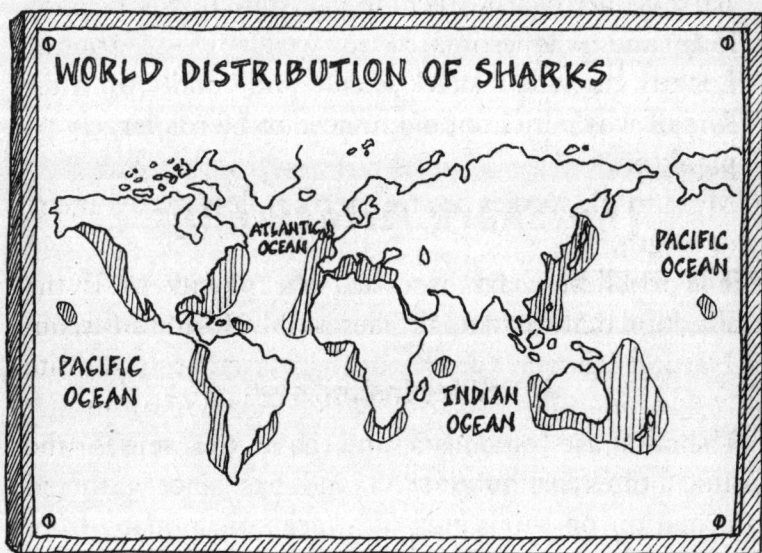

WORLD DISTRIBUTION OF SHARKS

ATLANTIC OCEAN

PACIFIC OCEAN

PACIFIC OCEAN

INDIAN OCEAN

Snappy facts

- Sharks are fish, not mammals like whales.
- Learning about sharks is a branch of ichthyology, the study of the physiology, history and importance of fish.

- There are about 368 species of shark, living in every ocean from the Arctic to the Antarctic.
- Sharks have no bones! Their skeletons are made of cartilage.
- Large oily livers help the sharks stay buoyant in water.
- The largest shark is the whale shark. There have been reports of these giants reaching 18 metres, but the largest ever scientifically measured was caught off Baba Island, near Karachi in Pakistan. It was 12.65 m long and was estimated to weigh 15–21 tonnes. Luckily the whale shark is cute and cuddly (in a big sort of way). It is not aggressive and feeds largely on plankton.
- Most shark species are tiny terrors, less than a metre in length.
- The smallest shark is called the pygmy or dwarf shark. A mature male measures only 15 centimetres.

Killer Instincts

All sharks are predators and have the senses and instincts of expert hunters:

Sound – Sharks use their hearing more than any other sense to home in on prey. They can pick up the sound of a struggling fish two kilometres away.

Smell – Sharks have the best sense of smell of any fish. They can detect one drop of blood diluted in one hundred million drops of water.

Sight – Sharks have excellent eyesight and can see things up to 15 metres away. Their eyes have a high density of cone cells in their retina and these are normally associated with sharp daytime vision.

Touch – Sharks have hundreds of sensitive pores in a lateral line on the skin along the sides of their bodies. These can sense vibrations and changes in water pressure.

Supersense – Sharks can detect tiny electrical charges from the muscles of their prey. They can even find their victims when they are covered in sand.

No Teething Problems

You have two sets of teeth and face years of visits to the dentist to look after them. Sharks are luckier. They have an endless 'conveyor-belt' of new teeth inside their jaws – as one wears down or breaks, a new one moves forward to replace it. Sharks can afford to lose thousands of teeth during their lives.

The Most Dangerous Sharks

Around twenty species of sharks have been known to attack humans, but four species have the worst reputations as people biters/eaters:

- The tiger shark.
- The bull shark.
- The oceanic whitetip.
- The great white shark.

Of these four troublemakers the great white has been blamed for more attacks than any other species. But this is open to argument. Some experts believe the bull shark is the real 'Mr Nasty'. It has larger jaws and is less fussy about what it eats.

The Great White

Do you like dogs?
Yes, but I couldn't eat a whole one.

OK, it's an old joke, but not to the great white. A medium-sized dog would make a perfect bite-sized chunk to this sleek predator. That's about the same as swallowing 200 quarter-pounder hamburgers in one sitting.

Chewing the Fat with a Killer

Great whites are superb hunters, honed by 350 million years of evolution to be perfect killers. They are intelligent, purposeful and know exactly what they are doing. Given the choice, they are also picky eaters, preferring a high fat diet. Favourite meals are seals, sea lions and porpoises. These mammals are insulated with blubber to protect them from the cold and are eagerly hunted as high-energy food sources.

If you are thinking of taking up scuba diving, here's a disturbing theory: to a shark's eye does a diver's black neoprene wetsuit make him/her look like a marine mammal, perhaps a seal?

Great White Table Manners

The great white carries its own 'eating irons' – triangular teeth with sharply serrated edges like steak knives. They are designed to slice efficiently through flesh, but if the joint of the day is a little tough that's no problem.

Shaking the prey from side to side gives a sawing action which can cut through tendon and bone.

When the great white attacks it doesn't mess about. The first bite is intended to disable the prey by causing massive blood loss. Sometimes a bite is so ferocious that a smaller seal can be bitten in half. But the sharks usually look closely before swallowing. Naturalists have seen them spitting out less tasty nibbles such as a sheep's carcass or a surfboard.

Prehistoric Megamouth ... er ... Megalodon

Fifty million years ago a relative of the Great White shark ruled the seas. Fossil teeth are all that remain of this giant predator – and what teeth! Some measure almost 18 centimetres, more like daggers. Using these it is possible to estimate the size of the ancient shark – a whopping 14 metres, at least twice as long as the great white. No wonder it was given the name megalodon – 'mega' indeed.

Conservation Concerns

Sharks give humans the shivers, but is this a fair reputation? What are your chances of being eaten by a shark?

Reassuring Thought 1

About 80 per cent of shark species have never attacked a human being.

Reassuring Thought 2

In the USA, the risk of being zapped by a bolt of lightning is 30 times greater than that of being attacked by a shark.

Reassuring Thought 3

Far more people are injured driving to the beach than by sharks in the water when they get there.

The Big Reassuring Thought

Each year billions of trips are made by people to have fun in the sea – surfing, sailing, diving, fishing. Yet worldwide only 70–100 injuries are reported each year, causing 5–15 deaths. The number of shark attacks is going up but that is because of vastly increased human activity in the shark's natural environment.

Mistaken Identity

Humans are only occasional visitors to the sea, so they are not on the favourite snack menu of sharks. In fact, people are bitten because they are in the wrong place at the wrong time and are mistaken for food, such as seals. Sharks usually attack from below, looking for targets silhouetted against the light. Human victims have included swimmers, surfboarders and divers.

Jaws Author Eats His Words

Have you read the book *Jaws* or seen the Steven Spielberg film of the same name? Remember the music – der-der-der-der – which accompanied the menacing fin cutting through the waves? Creepy! In 1999 the author,

Peter Benchley, apologized to great white sharks every-where. He admitted his novel had portrayed them as monsters and terrified the public. What's more, he owned up that when he started writing the book in 1972, 'There was little known about this animal.' He said, 'I read everything that was available and made up the rest. That's the advantage of fiction.'

Now he has changed sides and is working to help conserve the great white. Peter added, 'I want to use every medium at my disposal to show that the villains today are the people and not these fish.'

Top naturalist Peter Klimley from the University of California commented, 'I think Peter has got a con-science now . . . It is late, but better late than never.'

Sharks' Fin Soup – A Recipe for Extinction?

At worst, sharks kill 15 to 20 people a year. Yet nobody knows for certain how many sharks are killed by people. Some estimates are as high as 100 to 150 million a year. This is a tragedy of enormous proportions. Sharks are slow-growing, mature slowly and do not reproduce in large numbers. Human hunting is driving sharks to the brink of extinction.

And what seems really crazy is that many of them are killed for . . . SOUP!

Sharks' fin soup is a popular oriental meal and demand for fins is high. The stringy tendrils from dorsal, pectoral and lower tail fins are the choice ingredients of this expensive delicacy. Long-line fishermen lay out miles of baited hooks to catch tuna and other fish. Amongst their most valuable victims are sharks. Sadly the trade not only threatens shark populations, but is cruel and wasteful. When the fins have been cut off the carcass is thrown overboard.

The great white shark is now a protected species in South Africa, California, South Australia and Tasmania – but it is the only species of shark to be looked after by law. This is only the beginning of a long battle.

Crocodiles

Picture this idyllic scene: you are snorkelling happily in the warm Pacific Ocean, off the coast of Western Australia. Suddenly a 3 metre crocodile clamps its jaws on your head. What do you do next, besides scream, cry and yell? There is only one way to stop this armoured assassin. For a life-saving lesson start turning the pages.

Crocodile Attack Reports

Attack Report 1: African Lizards on the Loose

In the 1990s, Malawi in Africa became a success story for Nile crocodile conservation. The country signed the Convention on International Trade in Endangered Species (CITES) and reduced its crocodile trade. Traditionally, 800 or more crocodiles were killed annually. One hunter, Khaled Hassan, estimated he had killed 17,000 since 1963. Their hides went to the fashion houses of France while the meat was sold as a delicacy. Malawians, especially those living abroad, love the taste of croc tail. It reminds them of home. After Malawi signed up to CITES the annual cull dropped to 200.

In the new millennium, however, some Malawians are wondering if they have been too kind to the reptiles. The crocodile population is booming and so are attack reports. In the south of the country, in the Lower Shire Valley, Khaled estimates that at least two people are killed every day. And what's more, deaths are so common that some are not even reported to the police.

There is trouble in the north too. In early May 2000 a woman in Nkhota Kota had gone to collect water. As she bent down by the lake a croc grabbed her arm and tried to drag her under. Passers-by rushed to her rescue and pulled her clear, but not before she was badly injured. Locals blamed a lakeside sugar company that also ran a crocodile farm. When new management took over they closed the farm down, and some believe they turned the unwanted animals loose. Just what you need on your doorstep – sweet-toothed crocs on the look out for a meal.

Attack Report 2: Ramree Island

Most attacks by crocodiles on humans involve just one or two animals. An unwary person might be snatched from the shore or dragged into a swamp. During World War II, however, ferocious jungle warfare gave the saltwater crocs of Burma a rare feast.

In 1945 the tide of war had turned against Imperial Japan. The sweeping advance that had brought tough Japanese soldiers to the borders of India was over. Slowly, bloodily, British, Australian and Indian troops pushed them back through the jungles of Burma. In February a large force of Japanese soldiers were cut off on Ramree Island, close to the Burmese coast in the Bay of Bengal. In a desperate attempt to escape, they retreated into a huge mangrove swamp, hoping to be picked up by their own ships. Instead, the Japanese were trapped. The British opened up with artillery and mortars but when darkness fell the crocodiles moved in . . .

Bruce Wright, a naturalist before he joined up, was a member of the British forces who surrounded the Japanese. He was sitting on a marine launch, which had run aground on the mud of a channel. This is his account of what happened next:

It was the most awful night that any of the M.L. (motor launch) crew had gone through. Between the scattered rifle shots in the pitch dark, the screaming of men was heard as they were crushed by the jaws of huge reptiles. Almost as alarming was the devilish cacophony of crocodiles turning around. At sunrise the vultures came to clean up the human remains. Of almost 1,000 soldiers that entered the swamps of Ramree, only about 20 survived that night.

If this story is accurate it is by far the worst crocodile attack on record. But some experts now have doubts. Crocodiles are not bullet-proof, no matter how big they are. How could nearly a thousand armed men have been killed? It seems more likely that many died from shellfire and were eaten afterwards, while others managed to escape.

Attack Report 3: Tourist Terror

Bet you think you are safe from crocs in a zoo? Well, you probably are, if you have half a brain. They stay in their pit and stare grumpily at you, while you watch them from outside – right? And if by any chance you drop something in the pit – a bag, wallet or camera maybe – you think:

'Oh dear, tough luck', or 'I'll go and get the help of a zoo-keeper'.

But some people are just plain stupid.

In December 1999, tourist Sean Durie, aged 23, was visiting the zoo on Fuerteventura in the Canaries. When his sunglasses fell off he clambered over the fence into the croc pit to get them. YES, REALLY. Then as he tried to climb out he slipped down the muddy slope towards the crocodile's pool – where 20 crocs basked peacefully in the sun. Again and again Sean tried to scramble out, even taking his mud-encrusted trousers off because they were weighing him down.

Fortunately for Sean, his girlfriend, Sarah, ran to fetch the keepers. Now zoo-keepers are generally sensible folk. They took one look at this crazy tourist and decide not to climb in after him. Instead they threw him a pair of boots with a good grip and waited for him to crawl up the slope and climb back over the fence.

When Sean got out was he abashed? No, not Sean. He thought he was a bit of a hero and told a reporter:

'I stood up to make myself as big as possible and looked them straight in the eye. Amazingly it worked. They didn't start snapping until I was safe on the bank.'

If only someone had interviewed the crocs. What might they have said:

'It was the best laugh we've had for weeks. Watching him scramble up and down the pit sides. And when he took his trousers off . . .'

Attack Report 4: Boy v. Croc

Friday, 22 September 2000 was a great day for Australian 12-year-old Sam West. His dad, Bill, was a prawn fisherman and owned his own trawler, the *Amanda Lee*. It was the holidays and father and son were spending rare time together on the boat.

With the boy aboard, Bill West decided to take it easy. *Amanda Lee* was anchored near Montilivet Island, off the Kimberly Coast of Western Australia. The crew were ashore, soaking up the sun on a deserted beach, while Sam snorkelled back and forth, about 20 metres from the shore. A good day. Too good!

Think about snorkelling for a moment. You swim along face down, fascinated by the vivid sealife visible through your mask. Unless you raise your head you can't see what is happening around you. Your ears too are under the water and you can't hear clearly. You are skimming along the edge of a strange environment. Exciting!

Hardly surprising then that Sam had no warning that a 'salty', a saltwater crocodile, was homing in fast. Normally crocs live in the brackish waters of tidal rivers – but they don't have to stay there. Crocodiles are brilliant swimmers and quite at home in the open sea. The croc, attracted by Sam's splashing and flat posture in the sea, reckoned he was a tasty meal – maybe a big fish or small dolphin. It closed the last few metres in a flash and locked its teeth around his head.

A boy against a crocodile is hardly a fair fight. Sam was unarmed, skinny – half grown. The croc was 3 m long, covered in thick horny armour and weighed about 120 kilograms. But boys have an instinct to survive. There's only one place to hurt a croc with bare hands – the eyes. Without thinking Sam hammered and gouged at the animal's raised eye sockets. Shocked, the crocodile let go, bit again and again on Sam's arms and hands – and then gave up. This prey was too much hassle. The attack was over in seconds.

The men on shore heard Sam's screams and rushed to his aid in a dinghy. But by the time they reached the boy, the attack was all over. A float plane was called in to pick Sam up and he was flown to hospital in Darwin.

Once there he was cleaned up and treated for lacerations to the head, wrists and hands. Later Bill West proudly told a reporter:

'The croc gripped Sam four or five times. He's very, very lucky to be alive. He's one very gutsy little boy.'

Survival Guide: In a While, Crocodile

If you don't want to become reptile food, follow these guidelines to stay safe in croc country:

- Don't feed crocodiles. (Yes, people REALLY do.) Many attacks involve crocodiles that have been fed and lost their fear of humans.
- If you are fishing, don't dump fish scraps into the water. The refuse will attract crocodiles.
- If you are on a boat, don't trail a leg or arm in the water. The limb could make a tempting morsel.
- Crocodiles are silent and deadly hunters. Stay at least 3 metres away from the waterline.
- Be sure to check the water before swimming. Don't let children paddle or play in the water if you have the slightest doubts about safety. And keep your dog on dry land too.
- Don't swim or fish near heavy vegetation, it may be a hiding place for a crocodile.
- Don't go out in the dark without a torch. Most attacks happen at night. Crocodile eyes light up in a torch beam.

- Don't go close to a croc. Stay at least 25 metres away. Remember they can move fast on land.

Worst Case Scenario: Fighting Back

- If a crocodile corners you on land, try to climb on its back and push its neck downwards. This will force its head and jaws down, so it can't snap at you.
- Copy Sam West! If you have to fight, go for a crocodile's eyes. Sometimes even covering a reptile's eyes will make it more sedate and give you the chance to get away. Oh, by the way, the nose is pretty sensitive too.
- If a reptile gets you in its jaws, don't let it shake you or roll over. This can cause severe tissue damage. The best thing to do is to try to keep the reptile's mouth clamped shut so it can't get a grip on you in the first place. Surprisingly this isn't too difficult. Although crocs have powerful muscles for snapping their jaws shut, the muscles for opening their jaws are fairly weak.
- If you are bitten, seek medical attention straight away. Crocodiles have nasty germs in their mouths.

Crocodile Tales

- The study of crocodiles is called herpetology.
- Crocodiles are the oldest predators in town. Based on fossil records, scientists estimate that they have been around for 200 million years. They have outlived dinosaurs by 65 million years.
- All crocodiles are predators and several species have been known to attack people. The Mugger crocodile

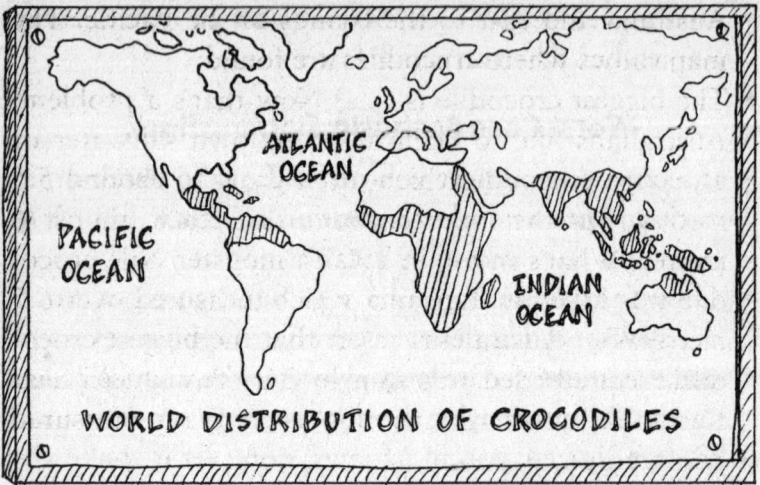

WORLD DISTRIBUTION OF CROCODILES

(Indian subcontinent), the Orinoco crocodile (Columbia and Venezuela) and the American crocodile (Southern USA, Central and South America) will all grab a human being if they get too close and there's nothing better to do on a hot evening. But the champion maneaters, by far, are saltwater crocodiles which attack around 2,000 victims a year and their old rival, the Nile crocodile, which attacks around 1,000 victims a year. Statistics like these make mammal predators, such as the tiger, seem like amateurs.

- The Nile crocodile is not only found along the river Nile but throughout tropical and southern Africa and Madagascar, in rivers, freshwater marshes, estuaries and mangrove swamps. The estuarine crocodile is found in inshore waters from Cochin on the west coast of India, in the Sunderbans (see Chapter 4 – tigers live there too. Aren't the local people lucky?) across the Indian Ocean to New Guinea, south to

Australia and east to the Islands of the Pacific. The map shows where crocodiles are found:

- The biggest crocodile is . . .? Now that's a problem! Australians like to claim it's their own saltwater or estuarine crocodile which often grow to around 5.5 metres. But the Nile crocodile can reach almost 6 metres. What's more, in 1905 a monster Nile crocodile was killed in Tanzania which measured over 6.5 metres. But Australians assert that the biggest crocodile ever recorded was shot by Mrs Pawlowski near Karumba, northern Australia in 1957. It measured 8.64 metres.

Crocodilian Killers

Croc diet varies with habitat, but all crocs are carnivores. Adults will eat fish, crabs, lizards, snakes, buffalo, cattle, horses, zebra, monkeys and small hippos. In fact, almost anything, including humans.

Crocodilians are masters of the 'ambush attack'. Their tactics go something like this:

- Lie in wait in shallow water, near the shore.
- Stay hidden with only nose, eyes and ears above the surface.
- Wait until the prey comes within reach.
- Leap out at high speed, completely surprising the victim.
- Seize the prey, preferably by the muzzle or head.
- Pull the prey under water to drown it.
- If the victim struggles, spin or shake to tear off a piece small enough to swallow.

When a croc slides underwater its ears and nose close automatically. A transparent third eyelid, or nictating membrane, protects its eyes.

Croc teeth are conical-shaped and made for puncturing, gripping and tearing. Small prey are eaten whole while larger prey are torn apart. The croc digestive system is strong enough to dissolve bones.

In the 1860s in Natal, South Africa, one Nile crocodile bit off more than it could chew. This ambitious beast grabbed hold of the hind leg of a fully grown elephant at a water hole. Far from dragging the tusker in, the crocodile was hauled out and another member of the herd stomped it to death.

Crocs with Character

Kwena

One legendary Nile croc was Kwena from the Okovango Swamp in Botswana. This hungry charmer killed dozens of people before it was shot by hunter Bobby Wilmot in 1968. Kwena was 5.8 m long and weighed about 816 kg. When its stomach was slit open out tumbled two goats, half a donkey and the clothed torso of a woman. Yuk!

Sweetheart

Crocs don't just attack people because they are hungry, they may strike because they are defending their territory. This probably explains the behaviour of one of Australia's most famous 'salties'. In the 1970s Sweetheart lived in Sweet's Lookout Billabong, on the

Finnis River, Northern Territory. He was 5.5 m long and weighed 816 kg. And he hated boats.

The sound of an outboard motor brought Sweetheart out to do battle, like an ancient knight from his castle. In his time, he grabbed more than twenty engines in his jaws and even sank a small boat or two by ripping their hulls open. Although he never injured a human, local fishermen threatened to shoot the crocodile and state rangers decided to take action to save him. He was to be sedated and moved to a wilderness area, but the plan sadly went wrong. When Sweetheart was shot with an anaesthetic dart, he became trapped under a log and drowned. His stuffed body can still be seen in Darwin Museum.

An Ideal Pet? Not Likely!

Crocs can become quite tame. A doctor in Villavicencio, Columbia, kept an Orinoco crocodile as a pet. He had raised it from a hatchling and it lived in his house. It was a female and grew to be 3 m long. Even so he let it play with his dog and children. On chilly winter evenings it liked nothing better than to lie in front of the fire.

Crocodiles, however, are not recommended as companions. They might be cute when they are tiny, but they soon grow. And even little crocs have a wicked bite. There are rumours that several American cities have crocodiles living in their sewers, unwanted pets flushed down the toilet.

In December 1999 undercover RSPCA officers in Britain raided a flat in Derbyshire to rescue Louis the alligator from life in a crate. He was the prize possession of a collector of exotic pets, but when he grew to 2 metres, neighbours became alarmed and complained.

Crunching Cousins

Crocs come from a big family – the crocodilians.

Crocodilian is the term used to describe the 23 different species of alligators, caimans, crocodiles and gharials alive today.

Alligators are the maneaters of the new world. The American alligator grows to up to 4.5 metres and weighs in at around 250 kilograms. Large populations are found in Florida and the coastal areas of Louisiana and Georgia. Compared to crocodiles, however, they are not big killers. In Florida there were only nine fatalities between 1973 and 1999. Most of the victims were children. Over the same period there were about 15–20 non-fatal attacks. The most dangerous month is May, the height of the alligator mating season.

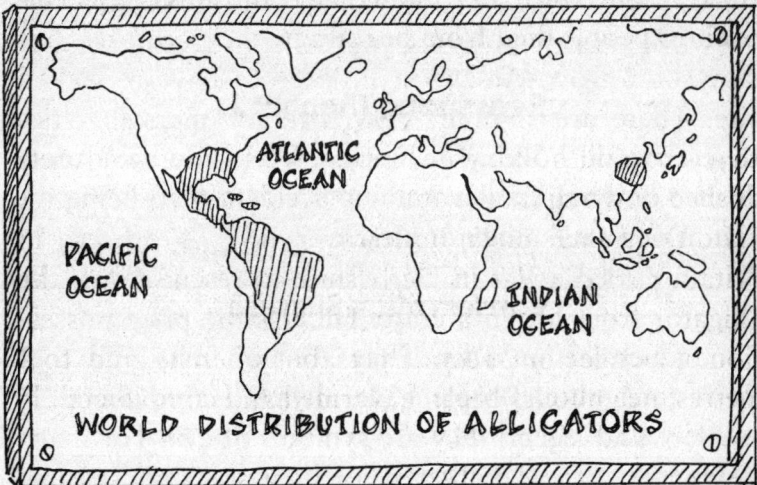

WORLD DISTRIBUTION OF ALLIGATORS

How do you tell a croc from a 'gator? Try this snout test:

- Crocodiles have long and tapered snouts.
- Alligators have short, blunt and shovel-like snouts.

Still unsure? Check again with the tooth test:

- Look out for the large fourth tooth in the lower jaw. When alligators close their mouths it is hidden, when crocodiles close their mouths this fits outside the upper jaw.

Conservation Concerns

Reassuring Thought 1

Only fourteen people were killed by crocodiles in Australia between 1973 and 1999. In the same period over 40 people died from bee stings.

Reassuring Thought 2

If you are on holiday in Florida, USA, you have more chance of dying in a swimming accident than being the victim of a fatal alligator attack.

Conservation Success

Crocodiles are unlucky. They are not furry and they don't look cute. People have always feared them. In folklore and legend they are symbols of evil. For many years they were slaughtered for their skins and treated as dangerous vermin. By the 1960s half the species of the crocodilian family were faced with extinction.

In the last 25 years, however, the crocodile has become a success story for conservation efforts. In the 1970s, all species were listed as endangered on the IUCN (International Union for the Conservation of Nature) Red List, a dramatic signal to the world. International trade in crocodilian products was regulated by CITES and over 100 countries signed up to save the crocs. Such international treaties have been backed by strong laws in individual countries like the USA, Australia and Malaysia. In the state of Florida, for example, anyone caught poaching an alligator faces a fine of $500 and up to 60 days in jail.

By 2000, sixteen of the 23 crocodilian species were no longer at risk. This was a far better record than had been achieved for any other wildlife group, including all the other predators in this book. However, seven species, including the Siamese and Cuban crocodiles and Chinese alligators, are still critically threatened.

Commercial Crocs

One reason for this outstanding success is that crocodiles and alligators are big business. The IUCN encourages the idea of sustainability. This means exploiting crocodiles and alligators as a natural resource, but making sure species do not become threatened by overuse. Hunting is allowed provided it is tightly controlled.

In the American state of Louisiana alone 20–25,000 alligators, mostly males, are shot or trapped in the wild every year and around 200,000 eggs collected

and sold to ranches. The ranchers then hatch the eggs
and raise the young alligators until they are ready for
slaughter, culling another 88–150,000 reptiles annually.
Throughout the 1990s an alligator skin was worth
around $25 and the meat sold for about $7 a kilo. Add
it up – lots of dosh.

Habitat Loss

The main threat to crocs and alligators today are no
longer hunters and poachers but developers and farmers. Most species need hundreds of square kilometres of
undisturbed wetlands – swamps, marshes, rivers, lakes
– to build up high populations. Yet all over the world
these are being drained, filled, dammed and polluted.

Florida is a notable example. The Everglades is a
top wildlife tourist attraction but these vast wetlands,
46,620 km^2, are dying of thirst. Since the 1940s a network of canals and dykes has been constructed to stop
floods and draw off water for Florida's booming cities.
A rescue plan has been prepared but it will cost $8 bil-
lion.

Amazing Immune System

One key argument for caring for other species is very
selfish. Humans never know when they might discover
something about them that we can use. Crocs and
'gators have been exploited for hundreds of years for
their hide, but now their blood may be about to come to
our rescue.

Researchers have long realized that crocodiles can
take a lot of punishment and still survive. In battles over

territory, males often tear legs and tails off one another. But amazingly, these severe wounds seem to heal up. American croc expert Dr James Perran Ross even found one poor beast with the whole of its lower jaw torn away. Nevertheless, this injury had healed and it was still swimming around and feeding.

In 1999, a BBC producer, Jill Fullerton-Smith, made a brilliant observation. She noticed that badly wounded saltwater crocs hardly ever had infected wounds. This was a major reason they could recover from horrendous injuries. What was going on? Jill and a lizard expert took croc blood samples and had them tested at New Jersey Medical School, USA. Scientists there split the blood into its component parts and discovered a substance that kills strains of deadly bacteria. They named it crocodilin. At a time when many antibiotics no longer work against superbugs, crocodilin is a new way forward for medicine.

Lions

When it's lunch time in lion land, who sets out to bring home the bacon (well, more likely a juicy antelope or buffalo)? Those magnificent males with their mighty manes? No way! They sit comfortably in the sun and wait for the lionesses to bring them a fresh kill. Even better, or worse, depending on your point of view, the males get first pick of the carcass. To find out more jaw-crunching facts about the King of the Jungle (or should it be Queen?) rip into this chapter.

Lion Attack Reports

Attack Report 1: Lions Attack Refugees

The Kruger National Park in South Africa is one of the finest wildlife reserves in the world. It is vast – the size of Wales – and is by far the best-run park in Africa. Unluckily for the Kruger wardens, the park's lions (and leopards) are learning to become maneaters. And there is little they can do about it.

The National Park lies along the border with Mozambique – one of the saddest borders in the world. Every year since the 1970s, tens of thousands of refugees have tried to escape war, hunger and unemployment in

Mozambique by sneaking into South Africa. In 1996 over 180,000 were caught and sent back. Thousands of the poorest and most desperate walk across the Kruger reserve – and some don't make it.

In July 1997, a ranger found 11-year-old Emelda Nkuna wandering in the bush alone. She had set off with her mother and two sisters but they had been attacked by a pride of lions. Emelda had hidden in a hole and listened as her mother had been eaten. Rangers found her mother's remains later, but her sisters were never seen again. In August, game wardens were forced to hunt and shoot a pride of five lions after they killed and ate four other illegal immigrants.

The park authorities have evidence that eleven people were killed by big cats (and five by crocodiles) during 1996–97. But Dr Willem Gertenbach, the Kruger conservation manager admitted: 'There's a good possibility

that many more refugees have died because we some-times find abandoned luggage and torn clothes. The big cats have not so much acquired a taste for human flesh, but developed an instinct that people on foot are much easier to stalk and catch than, say, an impala.'

Attack Report 2: The Tsavo Maneaters
(The greatest lion attack story – ever!)

On 1 March 1898, Lieutenant Colonel John Henry Patterson arrived in Mombasa, in what is now Kenya. He had been hired to act as engineer on the building of a tricky railway bridge across the Tsavo River (pro-nounced SAH-vo). He also had a reputation as a hunter. It was just as well. Game was short on the African plains that year and the lions were hungry.

What a rotten job
No sooner had John taken charge, than a series of appalling attacks by big cats began. And his workers were the victims. Most of the men had come from India hoping to earn a decent wage but they found nothing but misery in Africa. They lived in camps strung out along 30 miles (48 kilometres) of railway and spent their nights in terror – the hours of darkness became the killing hours.

The first of John's men to perish was a man called Ungan Singh. He and several other workers were asleep in a tent, with Ungan bedded down next to the flap. Without warning, a lion stalked in and dragged the man away. He fought back, bravely battering at the beast's neck, but stood no chance. The next day John and a hunting party followed a grim track in the sand – the victim's heel marks and pools of blood. Soon they found what was left of Ungan – bones, skin, scraps of flesh. And, most horrible of all, his head lying a few metres away, eyes fixed in a horrified stare.

After this the workers slept in fortified camps. They cut thorny bushes and built hedges, called bomas, to keep the maneaters out. Large fires were kept burning through the night. Everyone knows that animals are afraid of fire . . . aren't they? Unfortunately, the defences didn't work. The lions were used to hunting game through the thick Tsavo scrublands and they easily broke into the bomas, ignoring the fires. The death toll mounted steadily. No one knows for certain how many people the Tsavo lions killed in total, but the best guess is around 140.

As the attack reports were stitched together it became clear that two big cats were hunting as a team. When one made a kill, it shared the meat with the other. Eerily the railway workers claimed, neither had a mane, even though they were both males. Local Africans called them 'the ghost' and 'the darkness'.

Colonel Patterson waited, gun in hand, through many weary nights, but he was usually in the wrong place at the wrong time. If he patrolled one camp they would attack another. It seemed they almost knew his thoughts. In his darker moments even he began to worry that the lions were supernatural.

Strike!

At the end of November the Tsavo workmen rebelled. They angrily told John they would no longer be 'food for lions' and hijacked the next train to the coast. The few who stayed behind slept in trees or in underground pits covered with logs.

It was not until 9 December that the Colonel got the break he had been waiting for. An African came running to fetch him, yelling, 'Simba! Simba!' ('lion' in Swahili). One of the maneaters had killed a donkey nearby and was still busy eating it. Together, the two men tracked the big cat but as they crept up a dried twig broke with a loud CRACK. In a second the lion was gone, bolting into a dense thicket.

First kill

Intent on not letting the maneater slip away, John rounded up his remaining workers. Gamely, they agreed to surround the scrub and, beating pots and pans, drive the killer towards the Colonel. The plan went well until the lion broke cover. John held his own fears in check, lifted his double-barrelled rifle . . . aimed . . . and 'click' . . . the gun misfired. As the big cat rushed past, John blasted it with the second barrel. He was sure he scored a hit yet the bullet seemed to have no effect. Without even a shudder, the lion ran on.

Angrily, John wondered what on earth to do next. How could he bring the rogue animal to him and have time to take a careful shot? He thought it through. The lion had only just begun to tuck into the donkey carcass. There was lots of juicy meat left. It might just come back for a look. If only there was a tree nearby to sit in and wait. Then he had a really crazy idea.

John asked his men to build him an artificial tree – a shooting platform sitting on four stilts 12 feet (3.7 m) high. It was rickety but tall enough to keep him out of harm's way. Nearby, the donkey carcass was fastened with wire to a tree stump so that it couldn't be dragged off. As night fell, John settled down, alone, to wait for the maneater. But would it return? He didn't have to wait long. In the dark he heard a twig snap and a loud sigh of hunger.

Yet the lion ignored the donkey and circled the platform. The big cat had sensed danger and was stalking John. One swipe of its paw and the rattletrap structure would come tumbling down. In the tense minutes that followed he tried to get a bearing on the moving target. Then . . .

A growl in the dark!

In an instant John homed in on the noise, fired . . . and hit. The lion roared and crashed into a thicket. Undaunted, John pumped bullets into the bushes. The roars rose and fell as each one smashed home . . . and then silence. One maneater down, one to go.

Second kill

Eager to finish the job, John decided to try the platform trick again – using a dead goat as the lure this time. Once more the plan seemed about to work. The second lion turned up on cue and John took careful aim and fired. A hit . . . and a second hit . . . AND NOTHING. To his astonishment the injured beast ran away. 'Surely,' he thought, 'it must die of its wounds in the bush?' No such luck. On 27 December, the maneater was back, stalking a group of workers sleeping in a tree in the Tsavo camp. The cries of the men woke John and he fired into the dark. The maneater fled.

On 28 December, John, together with a gun-bearer, sat through the night in the same tree. At 3 a.m. he woke from his doze with a jump. The Colonel knew something was wrong. And sure enough there was the lion, slowly closing in on them, creeping from cover to cover.

This time, John fired at a range of only 20 metres. He couldn't miss and a direct hit smashed home. Growling in fury the lion ran away. John fired three times at the retreating animal and he was sure at least one shot was a hit. That made four direct hits! What was keeping this monster on its legs?

At dawn, on 29 December, John and the gun-bearer followed the bloody trail left by the lion. About half a kilometre away, they found it hiding in the grass. As it snarled defiance, John aimed carefully and fired and hit the target. Unbelievably, this wasn't the finishing shot. Pulling the last of its strength together, the lion flew at them in a rage. John pressed the trigger and the beast fell . . . got up again and charged. Astounded and terrified, John fired again, the seventh shot, and reached out to his bearer for another gun. He was out of ammo . . . and . . . no bearer. John glanced round to see that the terrified man had sensibly taken to a tree.

At top speed, John joined him in the branches, but he only made it because a bullet had shattered one of the lion's hind legs. Out of reach of the raking claws, John took the second rifle and fired once more. Thank God! The lion collapsed on this eighth shot.

In triumph John jumped down to look at the prize. Never in his life had anything been so hard won. Then to his horror it charged again. Furiously he cracked bullets into its head and chest. Yet, even in its death throes, the maneater bit savagely at a tree branch before it finally lay still. It had taken ten bullets to bring it down.

The dead feline point of view
It's enough to make us growl in our graves – if we had them. Our assassin sold our skins to the Field Museum of Natural History in Chicago for $5,000 dollars in 1926. (That's well over $100,000 now.) And we are still one of the museum's biggest attractions. So how come Patterson is the great hero in all this? OK, we were maneaters.

47

But ask yourself why? Had we any choice? Here are the real facts behind the Tsavo Maneaters Report:

In the 1890s, European settlers brought large numbers of domestic livestock – and their diseases – into Africa. One disease, Rinderpest, caused a terrible epidemic. This swept the continent and killed 80 per cent of animals with hooves – cattle, sheep, goats, antelope and buffalo. We faced a severe food shortage around Tsavo.

To make matters worse, it was hard to hunt the herbivores that had survived. There was thick thorny scrub everywhere. And why? Because humans had wiped out the local elephants for their ivory. Had there been ele-

phants near Tsavo, they would have eaten the scrub and opened the range up.

Who gave us our taste for human flesh? For hundreds of years slave traders abandoned their dead and dying slaves in our territory. We Tsavo lions had known for generations that people were good eating.

And then there was our painful dental hygiene problems. We both had badly broken teeth and had problems making a firm bite on the windpipes of our bigger prey. You humans were much easier to hunt than buffalo.

Be honest! What would you have done in our position?

Attack Report 3: Shaken Like a Rat

So what does it feel like to look death in the face? Especially when death comes in the shape of a lion? The great Victorian explorer David Livingstone found out when he was attacked. He wrote:

> *The lion growled dreadfully into my ear and shook me as a terrier shakes a rat. The shock caused a stupor similar to that of a mouse caught by a cat. It produced a sort of numbness during which I felt neither pain nor fear, although I was fully conscious. I was like a patient under slight narcosis who watches an operation on himself but does not feel the scalpel. This was due to shock which wiped out all feelings – even when viewing the lion directly.*

David was saved when his companions chased the lion off, but his account is curiously comforting. His mind had shut down to save him from agony. Interestingly, naturalists have observed that animals rarely struggle once a lion has brought them down. They think this is due to shock and that victims may not suffer as much as you might think. Easy for them to say so!

Lion Lore

- The scientific name for lions is *Panthera leo*.
- No one is sure how many lions there are in the world. Estimates range from 30,000 to 100,000 African lions.
- There is a second species of lions, *Panthera leo persica* or Asian lions. Only around 300 survive and they are confined to the Gir forest in India.
- Lions are social animals, often living in prides of three to fifteen, though prides as large as 37 have been recorded.

- Male lions in a pride work as a team to keep other males away from the females. At night the males patrol their territory, defending their turf with loud roars. When researchers have broadcast tape recordings of strange male roars, the loudspeakers have been attacked. A roar can be heard up to 5 kilometres away.
- Males are usually able to hold on to a pride for two to three years before they are driven out by younger and stronger animals.
- When new males take over a pride, they kill off any cubs the mothers can't defend. Around a quarter of all youngsters die this way.
- Lions are the second biggest cats, after tigers. An average male is 2.7 m long from nose to tail and weighs 157–180 kg. An average female measures 2.4 m and weighs 112–135 kg.
- The heaviest known lion was shot in South Africa in 1936. He weighed in at a hefty 313 kg. This was so big that the astonished hunters checked the figure several times on the local railway station scales.
- Lions are the only cats with tufted tails and male lions are the only cats with manes. A thick mane is good protection in a fight and attracts the females. You will have noted the Tsavo lions were maneless. They had adapted to the thorny scrubland in that region, where a mane would be nothing but a nuisance.

Have I Seen That Cat Before?

If you can't tell one lion from another take this ID chart next time you go to the zoo. Look out for these telltale features.

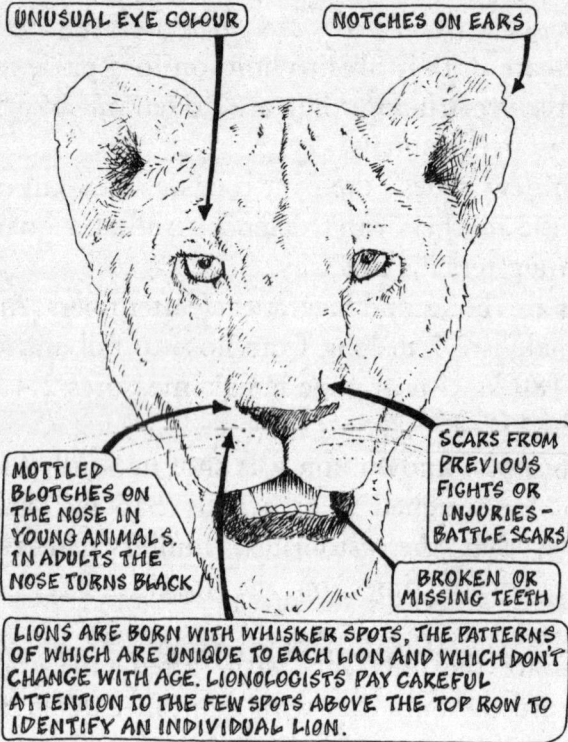

UNUSUAL EYE COLOUR

NOTCHES ON EARS

MOTTLED BLOTCHES ON THE NOSE IN YOUNG ANIMALS. IN ADULTS THE NOSE TURNS BLACK

SCARS FROM PREVIOUS FIGHTS OR INJURIES - BATTLE SCARS

BROKEN OR MISSING TEETH

LIONS ARE BORN WITH WHISKER SPOTS, THE PATTERNS OF WHICH ARE UNIQUE TO EACH LION AND WHICH DON'T CHANGE WITH AGE. LIONOLOGISTS PAY CAREFUL ATTENTION TO THE FEW SPOTS ABOVE THE TOP ROW TO IDENTIFY AN INDIVIDUAL LION.

Lion Lunch

At some time or other lions will eat almost any other animal, no matter how big or small. The list includes: locusts, mice, lizards, snakes, fish, tortoises, quails, zebra, warthog, hippopotami, rhinoceroses, young elephants and giraffes. An adult lion needs about 5 kilograms of food a day, though, like tigers, they can enjoy a good binge, eating around 18 kilograms at one go from a fresh victim. This may be followed by several days of sleeping and lounging around.

Remarkably for such large mammals, lions do not need to drink water every day. In times of drought they take moisture from plants, wild melons or the stomach contents of their prey.

Queen of the Hunt

Female lions do the hunting, often in groups of three or four if the prey is big or fast like a buffalo or an antelope.

In some prides, however, there are too many lazy lions. Lionologists call them 'cheaters', who watch others do the work and then join in the feast. If this happens too often the lionesses start to hunt just for themselves and their cubs.

Lion Attack Technique

- Hide in ambush, perhaps by a waterhole, or wait for younger members of the pride to drive the prey towards you.
- Pick a victim, look for a vulnerable animal – young, old or slow.
- Sprint to catch the victim by surprise.
- Jump on the back of the prey and dig in with needle-sharp claws.
- Drag down and kill. Choose from three favourite methods:
  a. bite the throat of the victim and crush the windpipe.
  b. bite the back of the neck and use large canine teeth to break or damage the spinal cord.
  c. swat with huge paws and cause internal damage.

If two or more lions are working together, one may grab the victim's nose and mouth while the others drag it down and rip open its belly. Sometimes the lions begin to feed while the prey is still alive. Don't get too upset, the victim doesn't live long!

Lion Table Manners

Lions have terrible table manners. They often fight over a fresh kill, but make up when they are full by licking one another's wounds.

Often there is a strict eating order: Males first, EVEN IF THEY HAVEN'T HELPED IN THE HUNT, then the females and finally the cubs. In times of shortage the males will eat their fill, even if the cubs and females starve.

When the prey is dead, lions usually start eating the contents of the body cavity first. Favourite titbits are the heart, liver, kidneys and intestines. The rest of the animal is eaten from the hindquarters, working towards the head.

Conservation Concerns

Lion Death List

Lions were once found in Europe, much of Asia and most of Africa. By the 1950s they had been driven back into African countries south of the Sahara desert. This list shows the lions' long retreat:

Country	Last known lion sighted or killed
Greece	c.AD 100
Pakistan	1810
Turkey	1870
Syria	1891
Tunisia	1891
Algeria	1893
Iraq	1918
Morocco	1920
Iran	1942

Asian Lion Crisis

By 1900 the Asian lion had been almost wiped out except for those living in the Gir forest. They survived because the local ruler, the Nawab of Junagadh, protected them for private hunting parties. As this book goes to print in 2001 they are threatened by a mysterious epidemic that is so serious the Indian state authorities are considering moving some of them to the nearby Barda forest range. To keep up with the latest news in this story check out the Asiatic Lion Information Centre at www.asiatic-lion.org.

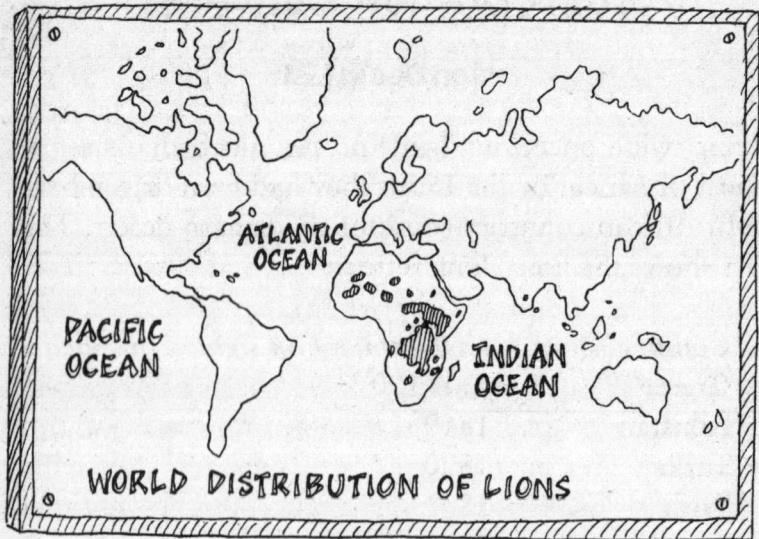

WORLD DISTRIBUTION OF LIONS

The Lions Have Stopped Roaring

African lions are not threatened with extinction but they are under pressure from human activities. Outside of national parks, like the Kruger or Kenya's Maasai Mara Reserve, they are becoming increasingly rare.

Africa has one of the fastest growing populations in the world. Huts made of a patchwork of mud, timber and straw spring up in days. Trees are cleared and new farms take over the habitat once used by antelope, zebra and buffalo. As prey becomes scarce, so big cat numbers fall. If the lions then start to eat livestock, such as cattle, they are shot or poisoned like dangerous vermin by worried farmers. Researchers have noticed a startling new change in lion behaviour: they are seldom heard to roar. The great predator knows the noise will attract human hunters.

Parks in Peril

Despite this, most African nations still want to preserve their wildlife as a national treasure. They have set up large game parks that attract tourists from all over the world and earn badly needed foreign cash. These reserves have been a great success and lion numbers inside their boundaries are healthy. But even here there are grave problems.

There are so many poor people in parts of Africa that the only way a man can provide for his family is to turn poacher. The main targets are elephants for ivory, rhinos for their horn, or game like buffalo for their meat. Often the raiders shoot lions because they are in the way. In some game parks there is what amounts to a small war between the poachers and the rangers. And the poachers are winning!

In recent years, as with Asian lions, diseases have been the main threat. The African lion population in the parks may be larger, but they are isolated and vulnerable to animal epidemics. And these are usually spread by human interference in Africa's natural ecosystems.

In 1994 rabies and distemper, spread by village dogs, wiped out a third of the lions on the Serengeti plains in

Tanzania and Kenya – over a thousand big cats. Video film of one of the first males to contract rabies shows the lion in its death throes: lying helpless, rigid and shaking, gripped by fits. Within 24 hours it fell into a coma and died. Between 1995 and 1999 the surviving lions and over 30,000 village dogs were vaccinated to bring the disease to a halt.

As one disaster eased, however, another had only just begun. By late 1998, 90 per cent of the lions in the Kruger National Park were infected with tuberculosis. This had been passed to them by buffalo – and the buffalo had caught it from cattle reared outside the park. Lions have no natural resistance to tuberculosis and the only way to stop the disease is to slaughter the buffalo herds. Over the next ten years most of the infected lions will die.

Tigers

Paws for thought: imagine sitting comfortably on the toilet in the frozen far east of Russia. Well, where else would you want to be? Bermuda? Suddenly you hear chomping sounds outside. A tiger is gnawing through the wooden walls. What do you do? To find out what happened to the real tiger outside the toilet, read on.

At best there are 8,000 wild tigers left in the world. Few ever attack humans yet, even so, these big cats cause more deaths than any other predator. Is their reputation as a sleek killer deserved?

Tiger Attack Reports

Attack Report 1: Malaysian Maneater

The people of the *kampungs* (villages) around Sungai Siput in Malaysia live on the fringes of the jungle. They have always respected nature and wild animals – especially the tiger, or *Pak Belang* as they call it. For them, the *Pak Belang* is an awesome symbol of strength and power – the 'King of the Forest' or 'Spirit of the Jungle'. Yet, they believe that the *Pak Belang* will not harm them so long as they stay away from its cubs. Usually an easy-going animal, if it could talk, the *Pak Belang* would say to humans, 'Hey, keep your distance. Let's live and let live.' But in June 1998 a rogue tiger was stalking the jungle – a maneater.

The tiger's reign of terror began on 16 June. Its first victim was a 46-year-old rubber tapper, Kamaruddin Noh. He was mauled to death on an oil palm estate near the village of Kampung Kajang. He was torn apart – and then his body was eaten. Three days later the beast struck again, killing Jais Long, 39, from nearby Kampung Jong. Bones and gnawed flesh were all that was found of both men.

In the following days the people of the area were stricken with fear. The children were kept away from school. The women no longer ventured into the jungle, not even to collect tapioca leaves to cook the midday meal. The men stayed home to guard their families or joined the hunt. No one went out alone. To stop the panic, teams of armed police patrolled the *kampungs*, their eyes warily scanning the thick undergrowth surrounding the settlements.

State wildlife rangers were called in to track and shoot the tiger, a team of fourteen experienced men. At first they tried to lure the big cat out of the jungle into a cage-trap, using fresh goat meat as bait. With young and hungry tigers this sometimes worked, but this one was too wily to fall for such an old trick. The job had to be done the hard way – days of exhausting tracking.

Twice, fresh pug marks (pawprints) were found inside the *kampungs*. It was almost as if the tiger was playing a game of cat and mouse with the rangers – taunting them before vanishing again. Eleven days after the first death, however, patience paid off. Two rangers sighted their prey, fired – and missed. In a flash the tiger was gone, escaping into the thick jungle. Now the rangers took a brave gamble – they followed it. Perhaps the tiger hadn't expected this, or perhaps it was simply too hungry, but soon they saw it again – eating the carcass of a cow near a stream. This time both men aimed carefully and the maneater was brought down by two bullets. The fierce and cunning jungle predator died instantly.

However, any satisfaction felt by the rangers was short-lived. Their job is to protect tigers, not slaughter them. They had even thought carefully before using live ammunition. Could this one be darted with a sedative and saved, perhaps in a zoo? Their leader, Sivanathan Elagupillay, had considered all the options and sadly decided the tiger had to die. He said to the press, 'It was a difficult decision for us but two lives had already been lost.'

A few days later, the rangers had good reason to be angry. Staff at the Malacca Zoological Gardens carried out a post-mortem on the tiger and the results were shocking. The animal was about 20 to 25 years old and had sixteen wounds on its body, some of them old gunshot injuries. Worse, the tiger's front leg was broken, probably by a poacher's trap. It could no longer hunt and had been forced to leave the jungle in search of easy game – humans or their livestock. The cruel actions of people had turned this tiger into a man-hunter.

Attack Report 2: Hero Dad

In December 1998, a ten-year-old Malaysian boy was attacked by a tiger in the northern state of Kelantan. Nasharuddin Abdullah and his father were near the edge of a palm oil plantation when the tiger pounced. It got a grip on the boy, who fell screaming to the ground. His dad, Ghazali, fought back at once. He told a reporter: 'I was shouting "Allahu Akbar" (Allah is the Greatest) and growling as I waved my hand to imitate a tiger.'

Astonishingly, the big cat let go and ran off. Nasharuddin survived, but needed 30 stitches. A spokesman for the World Wide Fund for Nature (WWF) in Malaysia warned that such attacks were likely to increase: 'We are developing a lot of land for farming and timber extraction . . . We are always saying the tiger encroaches into human areas. But we are the ones who are encroaching on their habitat.'

Attack Report 3: Trespass and Die!

On Tuesday, 19 October 1999, visitors to the Nehru Tiger Park at Hyderabad, India, found their safari trip only too real. Safe inside one of the reinforced vans, they toured the 40-acre park hoping for a glimpse of the magnificent animals. Yet, when the van neared four-year-old Rahul (a tiger born in the park), the driver, Srinvas, slammed his foot down. As he accelerated away a few of the startled visitors saw the reason why – and wished they been looking the other way. Rahul had attacked a human victim.

Only minutes earlier, eighteen-year-old Mohammed Khaja had been flying his kite. It had caught on top of the 6-metre wall surrounding the park and he had climbed up to free it.

'Get down, Mohammed,' his father had warned, but it was already too late. In a tragic accident he had slipped and fallen inside. As he lay stunned in the thick undergrowth, Rahul pounced.

Srinvas dropped his passengers quickly and, together with a brave set of park workers, rushed back to attempt a rescue. How would you feel about tackling a tiger unarmed? Srinvas and the others didn't hesitate because a life was at stake. At great risk, they drove off Rahul with screams and volleys of stones. Unhappily, their bravery was not rewarded. At Osmania General Hospital, the doctors confirmed that Mohammed was dead. Rahul had killed him with wounds to his head, face and chest.

Attack Report 4: Siberian Terror

Siberian tigers live in the far east of Russia. In February 1997, a Russian newspaper, *The Vladivostock*, carried this terrifying tale. When a local hunter failed to return home, a search party was called out which found his grisly remains. He had been eaten. A maneater was on the prowl and it had to be tracked down before it killed again.

As the search widened, tiger rangers checked a building site on the new Khabarovsk-Nakhodka highway and discovered tracks. This was hardly surprising in one way, since the road was cutting through tiger territory. But in another way it was alarming. Tigers hate noise and disturbance and usually they stay well away from construction workers. This big cat, however, had left prints near a site hut and, even more alarmingly, had gnawed the walls of an outdoor toilet. (The paper didn't report if anyone was inside at the time.) The worried rangers collected their rifles and set out in pursuit. They were on the trail but not quickly enough.

In spite of the news that a maneater was on the loose, a nearby trapper had set out to check his snares. His family tearfully pleaded with him not to go, but he brushed aside their fears. He knew the land, he said boldly, and had nothing to fear. When he was late, his father went to look for him. After a long search he came across his son, or at least what was left of him – two fingers, a scrap of scalp, a chain and a watch.

The rangers chasing the tiger found themselves in a marathon event. The hunt went on for two days before the big cat turned on them and was gunned down. When the rangers examined the body they saw that the poor beast had already been shot in the knee. It was another desperate animal that had been turned into a maneater by human cruelty.

Record-Breaking Maneater

The most infamous maneater was a fierce tigress known as Champawat. In the early twentieth century, she killed around 200 people in Nepal before crossing the border into the Kumaon district of India. But a change of scene didn't improve her habits and soon she had slaughtered human inhabitants.

When the British big-game hunter, Jim Corbett, was called in to deal with her, he found the local people living in terror. They stayed locked in their huts while Champawat roamed the countryside at will. In 1911 Jim tracked, cornered and shot the tigress. Champawat was a maneater that had to die, but even so Jim felt some sympathy for this ferocious killer. He discovered that her teeth had been damaged by an earlier gunshot wound. She had probably been in great pain.

Maneaters and Masks

The Sunderbans is the mangrove delta region of the Ganges and Brahmaputra rivers, on the border of India and Bangladesh. It is the best tiger reserve in the world, with around 600 big cats. Unhappily, the Sunderbans tigers have a grim reputation – as killers. As long ago as the seventeenth century, the French traveller François Bernier reported tigers swimming out of the mangrove swamps to snatch fishermen from their boats. And their eating habits haven't improved since. In a bad patch during the nineteenth century, 4,218 people were killed in just six years and until the 1980s around 50–60 locals fell prey to tigers every year.

In 1986 the Indian state of West Bengal tried a new idea to cut the number of deaths. At first it sounded – and looked crazy. Local people who worked in the Sunderbans were encouraged to wear a mask on the back of their heads. A mask on the back of the head? Yeah, that's really going to frighten a maneater!

OK, it might not have scared the tigers but it did make them cautious. The big cats usually attack from behind rather than head on. But that's difficult if you can't work out where behind is! In 1987, 2,500 local workers began to wear the masks – and not one was killed. And it wasn't as if the tigers weren't trying to find out what this new two-faced creature was. Several workers reported being tracked, one for as long as eight hours.

I DON'T KNOW IF I'M COMING OR GOING THESE DAYS!

Tiger Talk

- The scientific name for the tiger is *Panthera tigris*.
- In 1900 there were around 100,000 alive, divided between eight different subspecies, or kinds of tiger. Three of these were wiped out in the twentieth century and another is poised on the edge of extinction. The following table is based on figures compiled by the World Conservation Union (IUCN).

Tiger Numbers in 1998

Tiger Subspecies	Countries Inhabited	Maximum Number Alive
Bali	Bali	Extinct 1940s
Bengal or Indian	Bangladesh, Bhutan, China, India, Western Myanmar, Nepal	4,715
Caspian	Afghanistan, Iran, Turkestan, Turkey	Extinct 1970s
Indo-Chinese	Cambodia, China, Laos, Malaysia, Eastern Myanmar, Thailand, Vietnam	1,785
Javan	Java	Extinct 1980s
South China	China	30
Siberian or Manchurian	China, Korea, Russia	406
Sumatra	Sumatra	400

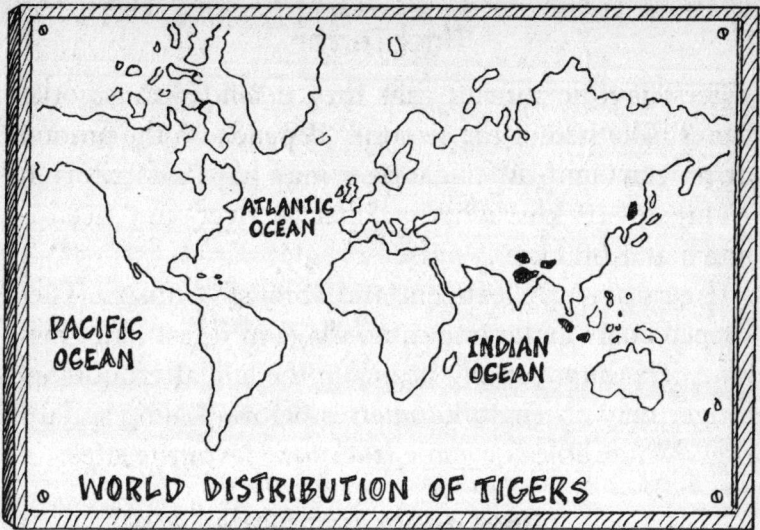

WORLD DISTRIBUTION OF TIGERS

- Tigers are the biggest cats in the world. The largest subspecies is the Siberian tiger. From nose to tail an average male measures 2.7–3.3 m and weighs from 180–306 kg. A male shot in Russia in the 1950s tipped the scales at 384 kg.
- The Bengal tiger is a smaller cousin, about 3 m long and usually no heavier than 230 kg.
- In the wild tigers live about 15–20 years.
- Unlike most members of the cat family, tigers love water. They are good swimmers and in hotter countries enjoy lying in pools and lakes.
- Tigers are solitary animals. Males and females only come together at mating time. A typical litter is 2–3 cubs, born 3–4 months after mating.
- The word for a group of tigers is a streak.

Tiger Terror

Tigers have territories that they defend against other males. The size of the territory depends on the amount of prey around. A jungle tiger may have a territory of about 25–60 km^2 while a Siberian tiger may need as much as 1,000 km^2.

Tigers are 'concealment and ambush' hunters. Their striped coats make fine camouflage in forest and grassland. The hunt usually begins in the late afternoon and a tiger may cover 30 kilometres before finding suitable prey. Water holes or game tracks are favourite sites.

Tiger Attack Technique

Follow these simple instructions and you can hunt like a tiger. (Try them on the bullies at your school and they are bound to leave you alone – if only because they'll think you've gone mad!)

1. Choose a young or weak animal.
2. Approach the prey from downwind.
3. Stalk from behind or the side.
4. Do not make any sound.
5. Close in slowly to about 20 metres.
6. Rush or leap the last few metres.
7. Seize the prey by the shoulder, back or, best of all, the neck.
8. Force it to the ground.
9. Kill with a bite to the throat and asphyxiate (choke) the prey or bite the nape of the neck and cut the spinal cord.

For a short distance, tigers can reach a top speed of 50 kilometres per hour. They can leap 5–10 metres from a crouch.

Probably only one in ten or twenty attacks is successful. If the prey escapes the tiger rarely gives chase.

Taking the Monkey

Observers have watched older tigers try this trick – a kind of tiger take-away. A senior tiger might explain it to a youngster like this:

'Well, my boy, walk quietly under a tree full of chattering monkeys. Of course they'll see you, but they think they are safe up there in the tree-tops. Let out a sudden roar, the full works, so that the sound carries for miles. Unless you are very unlucky, at least one monkey will be so shocked that it will let go of its perch. When the little fellow hits the ground, consume in one bite. Easy really.'

HMM, MONKEY SNACKS

Tiger Diet

- Favourite meals: deer, antelope, buffalo and wild boars. The bigger the better.
- Snacks, depending on the habitat: monkeys, birds, crabs, pythons, rodents, fish, frogs, jackals, badgers, bears, porcupines, people.
- Vegetarian alternatives: grass, fruit and berries.
- Problem meals (from a tiger's point of view):
  Buffaloes: Herds have often been seen working together to drive off a big cat. Faced with half a dozen charging bulls, a sensible tiger will look for easier game.
  Elephants: Tigers often come off worst in a fight with an adult elephant, but they will kill calves. In 1953 Jim Corbett watched two tigers work as a team to kill a large tusker elephant.
- Top tiger tip for tackling an elephant: if you are going to have a go at a pachyderm, rip its trunk so it bleeds to death.

Tiger Table Manners

Tigers like to eat in private. They drag their kill off to an area of dense cover, where the corpse can remain hidden from scavengers like jackals or vultures. A tiger can haul a 250 kilogram dead animal without difficulty, not bad when you think this is often more than the big cat may weigh itself.

In 1939 a tiger was seen to pull the carcass of a guar (a wild ox) for 4 metres. When it was chased away, thirteen men were unable to move the gaur.

A tiger can eat 20–40 kilograms of meat in one go, starting at the rump. If it is not disturbed it will feed from the same carcass for several days, until there is little left. Tigers that live in zoos eat about 5 kilograms of horsemeat a day.

So Why Do Tigers Attack Humans?

Tiger living space, in the wild and in national parks, is being squeezed. Tigers and people are simply getting too close for comfort. In India, where most of the world's tigers live, the human population has shot up by 50 per cent in the last twenty years. Sometimes villagers are struggling to survive and clear the forests to give themselves more farmland. Often businessmen cut the trees down for timber and then use the land for commercial crops such as sugar cane and palm oil. In 1999, the Malaysian government announced plans to clear about 7 million acres of forest for housing, industry, agriculture and other uses. Most developing countries have similar schemes.

Villagers often kill off pigs and deer in the forests near their settlements. These are the tiger's favourite foods. Starving tigers may be forced out of the forest to hunt humans or their livestock.

Old and injured tigers may attack people because they are easy prey. Once a tiger has acquired a taste for human flesh it is likely to kill again.

Conservation Concerns

Reassuring Thought 1

For every person killed by a tiger, 100 will die from a snake bite.

Reassuring Thought 2

In the course of his long hunting career, Jim Corbett shot dozens of big cats in India. Even so, he wrote:

Tigers, except when wounded or man-hunters, are on the whole very good-tempered. If warnings (growls, rushes and roars) are disregarded, the blame for any injury inflicted rests entirely with the intruder.

Taming the Tiger Killers

Until the 1950s tigers were seen as dangerous pests. In India the government paid a bounty for every tiger shot, while in China the Communist government outlawed the big cat as a threat to 'the people's food'. The Russians banned hunting in 1947 when numbers of Siberian tigers had fallen to around 30. But it was not until the 1960s that the rest of the world woke up with a jolt to the plight of the tiger – almost too late! The number of Bengal tigers was down to around 2,000.

In 1972 the World Wildlife Fund launched Operation Tiger and raised $1.8 million to back conservation in India, Nepal, Bangladesh and Indonesia. India began a huge rescue programme, Operation Tiger, supported by the then prime minister Indira Gandhi. With her support the tiger was adopted as the symbol of the country and 21 big cat reserves were set up. The tiger population in India bounced back to well over 4,000. Inspired by this example, other countries joined in. In Malaysia the tiger was upgraded to a Totally Protected Animal and the Department of Wildlife worked to safeguard tiger habitats. By the 1980s it looked as if the tiger was secure.

Counting Tigers

To understand if tigers are thriving or not, conservationists have to count them. Taking a tiger census isn't easy however. Unfortunately, they don't raise their paws to be marked present. Officials have to make a judgement of numbers from less reliable signs: pug marks, scratches on trees, sightings by locals, roars in the night, automatic cameras triggered by infrared sensors.

But some forest officers in India and Russia have been accused of fixing the figures. They claim there are more tigers in their reserves than there really are – so it looks as if they are doing their jobs well.

Conservation Crisis

In the 1990s, conservationists began to realize that officials might be tempted to fiddle the figures for a very serious reason – tiger numbers were falling rapidly again. By the year 2000, one-third of Siberian tigers had been wiped out, one-fifth of Sumatra's tigers were missing and numbers in the Indian reserves were less than 3,000. What on earth was going on?

Tiger Tonics

You've already read that sharks are facing extinction because of soup. If you thought that was daft enough, here's the sad account of what is happening to many tigers. They are being shot by poachers to make traditional Chinese medicines.

The Chinese respect the tiger as an awesome animal, but, unfortunately, many also believe that tiger body parts make potent medicine. Clock this medical time-bomb for tigers:

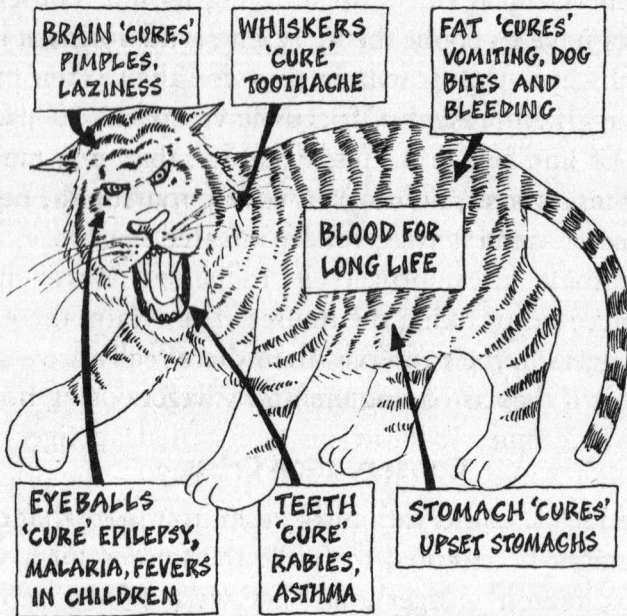

BRAIN 'CURES' PIMPLES, LAZINESS

WHISKERS 'CURE' TOOTHACHE

FAT 'CURES' VOMITING, DOG BITES AND BLEEDING

BLOOD FOR LONG LIFE

EYEBALLS 'CURE' EPILEPSY, MALARIA, FEVERS IN CHILDREN

TEETH 'CURE' RABIES, ASTHMA

STOMACH 'CURES' UPSET STOMACHS

This means that dead tigers are big business. Figures are hard to come by but South Korea has admitted that between 1975 and 1992, almost 9 tonnes of tiger bones were imported. Think about this. The bones of one tiger weigh roughly 10–12 kilograms, so it takes the bones of around 700–900 tigers to make 9 tonnes. The price per kilo varied from $127–250. The Chinese have revealed that 31,500 bottles of tiger wine and 15,000 cartons of tiger tablets were sold abroad in 1991.

Good News from Cambodia

Cambodia had been at war for 30 years until the late 1990s. Strangely, the fighting seems to have been good for wildlife. The war stopped development and tigers have bred safely in the jungles of the wild northern borders. In 1999 an American Group called Cat Action Treasury estimated that there were around 700 adult tigers in Cambodia. That's 500 more than expected, a significant boost to the world-wide population. Nice to have some good news for a change! Or did I speak too soon . . .

Not So Good News from Cambodia

There are reports of soldiers and villagers using home-made landmines to blow up tigers. A dead tiger was worth $1,500 dollars to a hunter in 1999 – the price of a Honda Dream, the most popular motorcycle in Cambodia.

Hard Hearts and Minds

It's all right for people from rich western countries to cluck and fuss about saving tigers, but we don't live next to them. Many farmers near tiger ranges and parks live hard lives and resent big cats that prey on their animals – or even their families. The farmers are often banned from the reserves and see good land going to waste.

The Russian newspaper *The Vladivostock* summed up the problems of living with big cats in 1997:

> *The tiger is not simply threatened by poachers who sell hide and body parts for 'medicine'. A deeper threat is the hatred rural people feel for tigers. The great cats may be beautiful, but they are also dangerous predators, every year someone is killed by a tiger. Some hunters and trappers freely admit that they have shot tigers and left them to rot in the woods . . . It would be nice if men and tigers could become friends in the wilds. But such thoughts seem hopelessly optimistic when one considers the savagery of men and tigers.*

The Ice Bears

Have you heard this version of the children's rhyme:

> *Row, row, row your boat,*
> *Gently down the river,*
> *If you see a polar bear,*
> *Don't forget to shiver?*

There is hidden wisdom here. If you are caught out in a small boat with a polar bear closing in – row, row as fast as you can in the opposite direction. An adult male polar bear weighs around 400 kilograms, swims like a fish and could smash your boat with a single blow of its 30-centimetre webbed paw. So how dangerous are they? Some attack stories are truly terrifying.

Bear Attack Reports

Attack Report 1: Seismic Situation

Tony Overton snuggled into his sleeping-bag and relaxed. He reached out and patted the rifle by his right side. He hadn't seen a whisker of a bear but it was comforting to know the weapon was to hand. Just in case. It was 1 July 1961, and the Arctic sun shone through the night. A perfect time to sleep on the ice.

Tony and three colleagues from the Canadian Department of Energy were doing seismic studies (checking on movement in the ground) on the sea ice off the coast of Ellef Ringes Island. Usually the four men shared a large tent but one of them had spilt some water in it and soaked the groundsheet. Tony and two others decided to sleep outside. If they had tried it in winter, when temperatures plunged to −40° C or below, they would have frozen to death in minutes. But this was midsummer and the prospect of a night in the open was almost a pleasure. They tugged their gear outside and were soon sound asleep.

Have you ever had the feeling you were being watched? Swung round suddenly to see who might be creeping up behind you? Some say this is an ancient instinct, from the time humans were just another species of wary primates on the look out for predators. Well, at around 4 a.m. Tony snapped awake – a huge alarm bell ringing in his head.

As he looked around he saw a bear about 65 metres away – and closing fast. Polar bears may not be built for a marathon, but they can sprint. Tony reached for his rifle but before he could lift it the beast was on him. Desperately, he raised his hand to protect his face – and probably saved his own life. Polar bears usually hunt seals and kill them with a crushing bite to the head or neck. Instead, the bear caught Tony by the arm and hauled him out of the sleeping-bag.

For a second he was too shocked to react and then he started to scream, long and loud. As anyone would, Tony expected his friends to wake up and leap to his rescue – but they didn't. In spite of the commotion they slumbered on. (One shamefacedly apologized later, 'Sorry, Tony, I heard you scream but I just thought you were having a nightmare.' With friends like these, who needs polar bears?)

It wasn't until Tony had yelled three ear-splitting times that Bill Tyrlik woke. It took him a moment to realize what was going on and then he lunged for the rifle. Yet the instant he moved the bear sensed danger. It dropped Tony and charged across the ice. With no time to aim Bill fired from the hip and in the luckiest shot of his life, hit the polar bear square between the eyes. It dropped at the end of his sleeping-bag – barely 2 metres away.

It seems likely that the bear thought Tony and the others, tucked up in their bags, were large juicy seals. It was no comfort to the men but the attack was due to mistaken identity.

Attack Report 2: Barge Bear

It was 1975 and two young oil workers were busy aboard a drilling barge, locked fast in the ice in the Canadian Beaufort Sea. It was a bitter, Arctic winter night and they decided to take a coffee break in the mess hall. They set off together, walking in single file along the narrow decks, but one never arrived. For a few minutes his companion wasn't worried, perhaps the other had forgotten something and turned back to fetch it. But the Arctic is unforgiving and workers are cautious and soon the alarm was raised. In minutes the crew had searched the barge bow to stern and what they found was deeply worrying – claw marks on the door of the sewage plant where the lost man worked. It was a bear attack.

At midday, when the darkness lifted a little, a grim sight met their eyes. The head of the missing oil worker was lying on the ice and a trail of blood led off into the gloom. Bravely a search party set off in pursuit of the rogue bear and found it nearby – crouching over their companion's partly eaten body. One recalled:

> *We tried firing a flare gun, but it froze up. The bear would stand up and shake the body like a dog with a wood chuck (stick). We chased him with a fork-lift but he moved off into the jagged ice where we couldn't follow.*

There wasn't a rifle aboard the barge and the traumatized men had to wait until a police gun was flown in before the bear was shot. There wasn't a lot of their fellow worker to recover by this time.

Attack Report 3: Canadian Hotel Horror

One night in 1983 a homeless man was raking through the wreckage of a newly burned out hotel in Churchill, Manitoba. He thought his luck was in when he found some unspoiled meat in a freezer and stuffed it in his pocket. It was to cost him his life. Unfortunately a polar bear was scavenging through the same ruins and caught the scent of the meat.

The bear attacked and clamped its jaws around his head, shaking him like a rag doll. Woken by his screams of agony, nearby residents rushed out in their nightclothes to help. They shouted at the bear and chased it with broomsticks. But it held on with a vice-like grip. By the time the polar bear was shot, its victim was dead.

Survival Guide: Bear This in Mind in Polar Bear Country

You never know when this advice from the Arctic Ecosystem Team in Alaska might come in handy.

Avoiding Bear Attacks

- Be alert. You can never be sure what a polar bear will do and spotting one early cuts the chances of a dangerous encounter.
- Keep a clean campsite. Make sure there are as few food and rubbish smells as possible.

- Carry a weapon and travel in a group.
- Do not approach a bear to take a photograph.

If a Bear Comes Near

- Get into a vehicle and drive away.
- Do not run. Stand your ground.
- Drop a pack or item of clothing to distract the bear if you back off.
- Make yourself look bigger by holding a pack above your head.
- Shout or make a noise.

If a Bear Attacks

- Find safe shelter.
- Defend yourself.
- If the bear is a female get out of the way of her cubs.

Don't Eat the Bear – or, the Polar Bear's Revenge!

Several desperate Arctic explorers have made a deadly error in the past – they shot a polar bear and ate its liver. BIG MISTAKE! This organ is so rich in Vitamin A that it is poisonous to humans and they died!

The Bear Facts

- The scientific name for the polar bear is *Ursus maritimus*, that's Latin for 'Sea Bear'.
- Their habitat is the Arctic, where they spend most of their lives on ice-floes, but polar bears are international citizens. The five polar bear nations of the world all have Arctic territory: the USA

(Alaska), Canada, Denmark (Greenland), Norway
and Russia.

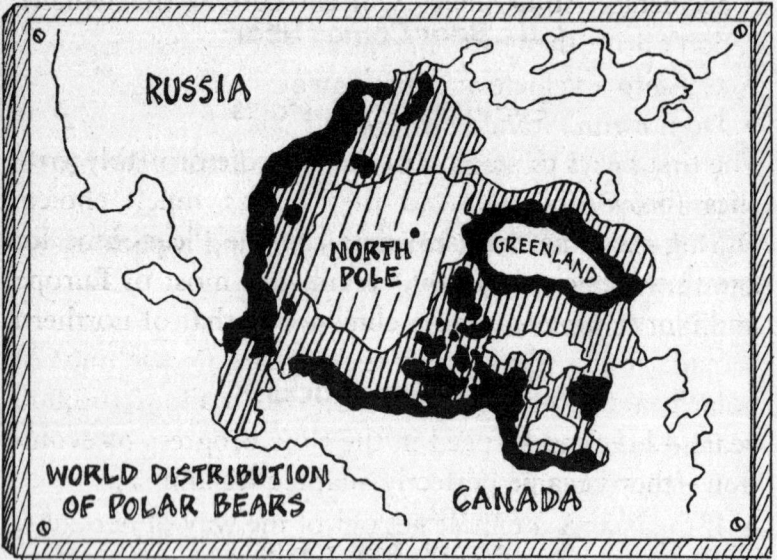

WORLD DISTRIBUTION
OF POLAR BEARS

■ NORMAL RANGE

▨ OCCASIONAL RANGE OVER ICE PACK

▧ OCCASIONAL RANGE OVER PERMANENT ICE

- Fact check: there are no polar bears in Antarctica.
- Male bears weigh up to 600 kg. The largest recorded
  was allegedly 1,002 kg. Females are a lot smaller,
  at around 104 kg to 250 kg. Polar bears are the
  world's largest land predator, twice the size of lions or
  tigers.
- In the wild polar bears live about 15 to 18 years. The
  oldest recorded male lived in London Zoo and
  reached 41.

- Females usually have two cubs at a time. Six out of ten cubs die in the first year from starvation or accidents. Adult males will eat cubs if the females don't drive them off.

Evolutionary Upstarts

The first bears to step on to the ice were probably grizzlies (brown bears). And they hadn't much choice. During the time that scientists call the Pleistocene ice age (1.8 million to 11,000 years ago) most of Europe and North America had a climate like that of northern Canada today. These ancient forebears ('scuse pun) of polar bears had to change to survive. In about 100,000 years – breakneck speed in the slow progress of evolution – they became perfectly adapted ice animals.

Adaptation 1: Fur

Most bears have black or brown hair. But everyone knows that polar bears have white hair for camouflage in a land of snow and ice. Right? Well, it's not quite that easy.

Each strand of hair is hollow, colourless and transparent. Their fur looks white because the hair is reflecting back visible light, the same way ice or snow does. At sunrise or sunset polar bears may appear golden – a magical sight.

But hollow hair can lead to problems. Look out for the amazing green bears! Yes really! Sometimes when polar bears live in zoos in warm climates, an algae grows inside the strands of their fur. This gives them a greenish tint.

Question: How do you turn a green polar bear white again?

Answer: Easy, wash the bear in a salt solution to kill the algae! But would you be brave enough to scrub under a polar bear's arms, oops sorry, forelegs?

Adaptation 2: Skin

Most bears have light skin under their fur. Polar bears have black skin to soak up as much warmth as possible from the sun. Believe it or not, they are so well adapted to the cold Arctic climate they often overheat. Surplus heat is released through body parts that are not covered in fur or where blood vessels are close to the skin – the muzzle, nose, ears, footpads, shoulders and inner thighs.

Adaptation 3: Swimming

Many types of bear are good swimmers, but polar bears spend so much time in the sea they are considered a maritime mammal. They have been known to swim more than 60 miles (96 kilometres) without rest – doggy paddling along at a steady 10 kph. A few bears have been sighted more than 50 miles from the nearest land or ice. Their massive forepaws are webbed to propel them through the water, while their hind feet and legs are used as rudders. A thick layer of fat under the skin helps them keep afloat.

Polar bears are skilled divers too. Their nostrils close when they hit the sea and they can stay down for around two minutes. Usually they swim about 3–4.5 metres deep but they can go to 6 metres. Their underwater vision is quite good. They can spot a meal at 4.5 metres. Sometimes polar bears dive to catch a bird resting on the surface, or to sneak up on a seal lying on the edge of an ice-floe.

Adaptation 4: Diet

Most bears would be perfect guests for your birthday party. They eat an omnivorous diet – a bit of anything really, if it smells OK – leaves, roots, fruit, fish, small mammals, carrion. Polar bears are much more fussy. They have become specialized hunters and at the top of their catch list is . . . seal.

Survival of the Fattest

In a hot history lesson do you long for strawberry ice cream? In a mouldering maths classroom do you dream of chocolate?

Don't blame yourself. You can't help it! Your prehistoric ancestors out on the African Savannah pre-programmed you to crave fatty food. It's a survival thing. Times have changed though. In today's fast food world overeating causes obesity and heart disease in humans.

But if fat is a problem for people, polar bears thrive on it. The rump of a healthy adult is insulated from the cold by a layer of the stuff up to 10 centimetres thick. This is so efficient they are almost invisible on infrared cameras that take thermal (heat) images as the layer of

fat stops their body heat escaping. So how do the bears keep up this layer of insulation? A high fat diet of course. And for instant gluttony there's nothing better than . . . seal blubber.

Enough to Make a Seal Blubber

Ringed and bearded seals spend most of their lives in the sea but they have to surface to breathe every few minutes. When the ocean freezes over, the seals make their own breathing holes, or aglus (pronounced 'ag'loo'), by scraping against the underside of the ice with their foreflippers. These have large, heavy nails, almost as big as a bear's claws. The seals become fond of their own aglus and keep them open as the ice thickens, until by mid-winter they become long tubes cutting through up to 2–3 metres of ice. The opening at the top may be as small as 15 centimetres.

Polar Bear Attack Technique

A polar bear can stalk a seal while it is resting on the ice, but this is hard work. They have a neater trick:

1. Wait beside a breathing hole. Be patient as it may take hours.
2. When the seal sticks its head out, seize it by the nose. Haul it on to the ice and consume while still warm.

A polar bear's neck muscles are so strong that it can rip a large 150 kilogram seal through a small aglu in one quick jerk – the victim's body crushed, internal organs pulped and the bones broken.

Puppy Fat

Seal pups make even easier prey. So if you like little cuddly puppy seals, with big liquid eyes, skip this paragraph.

Until they are weaned, young seals are reared in snow-covered birth lairs dug by their mothers. Unfortunately for them, polar bears carry a top-notch seal detector – their stunningly sensitive noses.

Check this out:

A fox can scent a quail at 100 metres.

A wolf can smell a wounded deer at 500 metres.

A polar bear can sniff out a seal from 32 kilometres (20 miles) away.

And once they get the scent, nothing stops them. Researchers in Alaska followed one bear as it set off in a straight line – across the tops of pressure ridges of uplifted ice – plunging through snow-covered passes, to reach seals 64 kilometres (40 miles) away.

So putting it bluntly, even though the pups are hidden they stand little chance. The bears pounce on the birth lair and break through the snow or dig the young seals out. When they eat them, however, most of the body is wasted. Polar bears go to all the trouble of killing seal pups just to get at the fattiest part – the lipid-rich brain.

Polar Bear City

The town of Churchill, in Canada, calls itself the 'Polar Bear Capital of the World'. The townsfolk haven't much choice really, they live on an age-old bear migration route. Each autumn the polar bears pass through, on their way from spending the summer in the forests to Hudson Bay and the seal grounds. If the winter is late, the bears can't hunt and spend their time roaming the streets looking for food. The town rubbish dump is a favourite lunch spot.

As you read in the Bear Attack Reports this can be risky, but the people of Churchill love their polar bears – not least because they are the focus of a thriving tourist industry. Bear-watching accounts for 60 per cent of the town's economy. In the bear season Tundra Buggy Tours fill 426 seats a day, seven days a week.

To cope with problem animals, Churchill built a polar bear 'jail' in 1982. It has 23 cells and no rations. It's usually females with cubs, and young bears with little experience of hunting, that chance a trip to town and end up in jail. The bears are tagged and flown north to the seal grounds.

Conservation Concerns

Reassuring Thought 1

In Canada, only seven people have been killed by wild polar bears in the past 25 years. In Alaska, USA, only one person has died in the past 25 years.

Reassuring Thought 2

In all of recorded history, only 21 people have been killed by polar bears in Russia.

Reassuring Thought 3

Most polar bear attacks do not result in deaths. If you make a loud noise, the bears back off. Many attacks are made by starving sub-adults (teenage bears) who are still learning to hunt.

Banning the Polar Bear Hunters

Native peoples of the Arctic, like the Inuit, have hunted polar bears for thousands of years. They killed them with a spear or a knife and used their bodies for clothing, sleeping skins and food. No work was done for four or five days after a successful hunt, out of respect for the soul of the dead bear.

Europeans had less regard for Arctic wildlife. By the nineteenth century thousands of bears were being shot for their 'luxury' fur. But it was not until after World War II that the crisis hit. High-tech hunting from snow buggies, ships, planes and helicopters amounted to a massacre. In 1965 the New York Times reported:

This kind of hunt is about as sporting as machine-gunning a cow. Its only purpose is to obtain the bear's fur as a trophy for the floor or wall of someone's den. The carcass is left for scavengers.

That same year, the Russians estimated that there were only 5,000–10,000 polar bears left in the world and asked other countries to help save them. In 1973 the five Arctic nations signed the International Agreement on the Conservation of Polar Bears and Their Habitat. In this they promised to share research, preserve the Arctic environment and ban hunting, except by local people using traditional methods. These measures have helped – the bear population has bounced back to around 40,000 animals. But there are other, perhaps even more disturbing, threats.

Signal from the Ecosystem

The Canadian Wildlife service has been studying polar bears in the Churchill–Hudson Bay area for more than 30 years. 80 per cent of the local adult bears have been tranquillized, tagged, tattooed, weighed and measured. Their blood has been tested, their teeth examined and their life history recorded. But, of everything checked, it is the bear fat that tells the crucial story.

Top polar bear scientist Ian Stirling measures bears using a body weight table. Once their weight has been measured, polar bears fall into five categories, based on their level of condition:

1. Bag of bones: basically skeleton hanging over a frame, maybe sick or starving.
2. Thin: spine visible under fur, feel pelvic girdle under skin because no fat.
3. Average level of fatness.
4. Very fat: when lying on stomach whole body ripples like a bowl of jelly when jiggled.

5. Obese: body practically round, belly and sides hanging down with fat when walking.

An average bear would measure three, while a pregnant female would reach five.

However, since the 1980s the mean weight of the bears is dropping. Young males, for example, are often are 80–90 kilograms lighter than they would have been fifteen years ago. Cubs are under threat too, more are dying and the birth rate has fallen by 15 per cent. The cause sends out a warning for the whole planet – polar bears are ice bears and the ice is vanishing.

Twenty years ago Hudson Bay was ice-bound, except for a very short summer period. Since the 1950s, however, the temperature has been rising by 0.3 to 0.4 degrees every decade. Now the ice breaks up as early as July, and with no ice-floes to hunt from the bears are forced to come ashore. They don't eat again until the freeze-up in late November. This is almost a month longer than normal.

Many scientists believe this environmental change is proof that global warming is a fact. If it is, then time is running out for the polar bears of Hudson Bay and the whole Southern Arctic.

NO ICE = NO POLAR BEARS.

Wolves

An eerie howl cuts through the night air. At first you think it's your mother singing again, but no, this is more tuneful. It's the cry of the wolf – one of the most spine-tingling sounds in nature. It is mournful, haunting and moving, but would you want a wild wolf pack living near you? In recent times, there have been no proven reports of any fatal attacks by wolves. However, in many parts of the world, wolves are making a comeback and there have been some near misses . . .

Wolf Attack Reports

Attack Report 1: The Walkers and the Wolves

On 29 June 1984, three scientists from the University of Toronto were walking in woodland about 15 kilometres southeast of Churchill, Manitoba. (Yes, the same Churchill in the polar bear chapter. Yep, they've got a lot of wild wildlife on their doorstep.) Peter Scott, Catherine Bentley and Jeffrey Warren were enjoying themselves and were more excited than worried when they came across signs of wolves – a criss-cross of paw marks and scats (droppings).

When they came to a nearby clearing the friends sat

down for a rest. It felt good to take their packs off and relax. Suddenly they heard a twig break, swung round towards the SNAP and came face-to-face with a cream-coloured wolf trotting straight at them. Are wolves dangerous? When they are that close not many people wait to find out. Catherine leapt to her feet stamping and yelling. In a panic, the wolf tried to stop and turn at the same time, lost its balance and crumpled into a bush not far from the startled scientist. Rolling to its feet it ran into the treeline, only to be replaced by another, bolder animal.

The new wolf was larger and distinctively marked with a black head and shoulders. It locked eyes with Scott and hurtled at him in great bounds – ears erect and tail flat out. Urgently scrabbling in his pack, Scott pulled out his bear horn and let off a blast. (A loud horn used to scare off bears – an accessory carried by many walkers in bear country in North America.) Stunned by the noise, this second wolf lunged to one side.

Now very scared, Catherine and the others raced to the nearest trees and shinned up out of reach. For the next four hours they were trapped on their roosts while a small pack of wolves skulked back and forth. One excitable animal unnerved them by barking, howling and whimpering at the opposite edge of the clearing. They wondered if he was annoyed at missing a good meal.

When they hadn't spotted a wolf for fifteen minutes, the scientists decided it was time to make a break. Dropping to the ground, they stood back to back in a loose triangle and moved slowly from tree to tree, all the way back to their vehicle. During their careful retreat, they blundered across a wolf den and guessed that the clearing might have been the pack's rendezvous site. Was this a wolf attack or had the pack simply been trying to chase them away from their territory? No one can be certain.

Attack Report 2: Alaskan Attack

In April 2000, the people of Alaska were shocked when a wolf savagely bit a child. It was the first confirmed report of a wolf attack in the history of the state. The victim was a six-year-old boy, at a logging camp north-west of Yakutat. He was playing with an older friend in a grove of alders when the wolf appeared. Alarmed, the boys stared at the animal, wondering what to do next. Well, what would you do? Yeah, they ran for it. As they turned, however, the wolf pounced. It knocked the

younger boy to the ground and bit him on the lower back and buttocks. It wasn't until a camp carpenter ran out and threw stones at the animal that it broke off the attack.

Ten minutes later, when the wolf showed up again it was shot. The body was burned in case it had rabies and the head was sent for examination at the University of Alaska virology lab. Fortunately the boy wasn't too badly hurt. He needed seven stitches and five surgical staples.

Attack Report 3: Cattle-Driving Wolves

How good a predator is the wolf? Cattlemen in the USA today fear they are very good. In their arguments against the reintroduction of wolves (see The Big Come-

Back on page 109) this incident has been retold as a warning. It was written by a Colorado hunter, called Elbert, in the late 1800s:

A few days ago while hunting antelope between Horse and Adobe Creeks I came in sight of a band of 30 or more wolves. They were herding about 200 head of range cattle. My curiosity induced me to remain a couple of days within seeing distance. They surrounded the gradually outspreading herd and chased the animals together. They would then await the motions of a leader who would run in, cut out a calf, when the rest would rush to help him throw it down and tear out its entrails . . . If any of the older animals hung back and showed fight they would be instantly hamstringed and left thus disabled . . . I am satisfied that the wolves and the cattle will be inseparable until the calves are all killed. Wolves behaving like cowboys – herding and killing cattle for several days. Now that shows real intelligence.

Protection Report 1: Guarded by Wolves

This report is different. Unlike the other predators in this book, wolves also have a reputation for kindness. There are a number of stories in which they seem to have adopted and protected abandoned human children. You probably know the most famous tale of all: Romulus and Remus, the twin boys raised by a she-wolf, who grew up to found the ancient city of Rome. Yet within living memory there have been similar reports.

101

During World War II, the Jews of Europe lived in terror. Misha was seven when the Nazis came to arrest her parents in German-occupied Belgium. In the nick of time, she was sent to a safe house but she never saw her parents again. Yet how safe was safe? One day she heard her 'new family' talking about handing her over to the Germans. They were frightened that if they were caught with Misha they would be arrested too.

Bravely, Misha decided to run away. And she knew which direction to head in too – she would go east into Germany to look for her parents. Guided by a tiny compass, she left after sunset. Food was hard to come by and she scavenged whatever she could – from raw meat to earthworms. One night, Misha was caught stealing food from a German farm and badly beaten. She was struck across the head and barely managed to crawl into nearby woods. Once she was hidden she let the pain wash over her and howled in agony.

A female wolf heard the sound of the child in distress and came to investigate. Far from attacking the girl, the animal took pity on her and brought her food. Misha called the wolf 'Maman Rita' and in the months that followed they travelled together. At night they slept fur to skin in a tight warm ball. The warmth of Maman Rita probably saved Misha from freezing to death more than once. For a time a male wolf joined them and they formed a tiny pack, with Misha treated as a cub.

Sadly, Misha's new security was not to last for long. Hunters shot the wolves and she was left alone again. Heartbroken, but undaunted, she kept on moving east into Poland. During the war, wolf numbers soared and

she found and joined a larger pack. Educated in wolf manners by Maman Rita, she was soon accepted and Misha stayed in the huge Polish forests until the fighting ended. In 1945, she walked back into civilization. After this Misha joined thousands of refugees who left Europe for America. She now lives in a quiet Boston suburb with her husband where she wrote her amazing memoirs.

Wolf Bites

- The commonest wolf is the grey wolf – also called the timber wolf, tundra wolf and the plains wolf. The Latin name is *canis lupus*. It looks similar to a husky.
- Wolves are the largest member of the dog family. A male wolf measures around 120–200 cm from nose to tail tip and weighs between 20–60 kg. Females are usually 15–20 per cent smaller than females. It is claimed that the largest wolf ever caught was 103 kg, but there are doubts if this record is true.

- All modern breeds of dog are descended from the wolf.
- Wolves rarely attack people, but wolf/dog hybrids are highly dangerous – they inherit a lack of fear of humans from the dog and the wild instincts of the predator from the wolf. One minute they can be the perfect family pet, the next they can turn and kill a child!
- Wolves can trot at 13 kph and keep up the pace for hours. They can travel over 150 km in a day if they need to. A wolf pack may have a territory of hundreds of square kilometres.
- Wolves have a double layer of fur. The outer layer is a natural moisture repellent. Breath won't condense on it – even on a freezing day. The woolly underfur is a perfect insulator, letting wolves sleep in the open at temperatures down to –40°F. They can regulate the temperature of the pads on their feet to just above freezing, so they can tromp over snow and ice with no discomfort.
- Wolves have webbed feet and are fine swimmers. What Catherine Bentley and the other scientists near Manitoba didn't realize is that wolves can climb trees too. They have to be pretty desperate, but they can do it.
- Reckon you have a good sense of smell? No chance! Wolves have a super hooter that is at least 100 times more sensitive than yours. So imagine how horrible your feet smell to a wolf! They can detect prey 250 metres away, if the wind is in the right direction.

Packing Them In

Wolves are social animals and exist as a pack. Packs can be as large as thirty, but most are seven-strong or less. The leaders of a pack, a male and a female, are called the 'alpha pair' by researchers. They are the largest and most intelligent animals and usually the parents of the others. The pups may look fully grown but they are still learning from their parents. Biologist Mike Nelson studied wild wolves near the American Great Lakes. He commented that wolf packs are 'highly organized, mobile nurseries'.

Top Dogs

Packs have strict discipline. The alphas are the top dogs. They stand tall, with their ears and tails erect. Did you know that staring a dog in the eyes annoys them? It's a challenge! Alphas deliberately 'outstare' every other pack member to show who is boss.

YOU'RE NOT TAKING THIS STARING THING VERY SERIOUSLY!

Underdogs

The subordinate wolves cringe whenever the leaders are near – crouching on bent legs, ears back and tails tucked between their legs. To show complete submission, an underdog must roll on to his or her back and allow the alpha to stand over them. You might have seen a pet dog behaving in the same way if it has been sharply ticked off.

Wolfing It Down

Wolves have a big appetite, feeding mostly on flesh and bones. Like other predators they can gorge themselves and then fast for several days. Depending on habitat, prey includes: reindeer, musk oxen, deer, moose, mice, rabbits, squirrels, fish and crabs, carrion – and if people are nearby, waste food.

Group Hunt

Wolves can hunt alone but they eat better when the pack kills as a team. A group of wolves can go after bigger prey such as elk, deer or moose. Wolves hunt by coursing (chasing) rather than stalking their victims like big cats.

Wolf Attack Technique:

- Pick a weak animal – young, old or sick.
- Chase and tire prey.
- Surround to confuse and terrify.
- Run to front of victim and bite nose or throat.
- Hang on until animal goes down.

Wolf fangs, the main canine teeth, can be up to 6 centimetres long. Imagine a set clamped on to the nose of a deer – a few shakes of the head won't throw this predator off. The jaws of a wolf can exert a pressure of 1,500 pounds per square inch. The pressure in a car tyre is about 30 pounds per square inch.

Have a Howling Time

Wolves woof, whine, bark, yelp and growl but they are best known for their eerie howl. Different howls carry different messages:

- 'Hey we're having a good time, let's howl.'
- 'There's another pack nearby, let's howl to warn them off.'
- 'Time for the pack to assemble, let's howl to let everyone else know where we are.'

In open ground, on a clear night, one wolf can hear another 13 kilometres away.

If you are in wolf territory and you howl well enough the wolves will answer you. Try this wolfie howl guide:

1. Build up your 'howl power' with two deep breaths.
2. Cup your hands around your mouth.
3. Tilt your head back towards the sky.
4. Let go with a long howl that rises up and slowly dies away.

Practise hard. Wolves don't like howls that break off sharply.

OK, your chances of talking to wolves may not be that good, but just think how much you can annoy the neighbourhood dogs!

Conservation Concerns

The Vanishing Wolf

Wolves were once found in more places on earth than any other mammal. They roamed the northern half of the globe, from the Arctic circle to the Tropic of Cancer. But for hundreds of years humans have trapped, poisoned and shot them because they were a danger to sheep and cattle. In folktales and myths, particularly in Europe, wolves became symbols of evil. Remember your fairy tales, *Little Red Riding Hood* and *The Three Little Pigs*?

The last wolf in Britain was killed in 1743 and in Western Europe most of the packs had been destroyed by the early nineteenth century. When Europeans migrated to North America they took their hatred of wolves with them and in most states a system of bounties was set up. In 1849 a dead wolf was worth $3 in Minnesota.

The Big Come-Back

In 1973 the wolf was finally protected as an 'endangered species' in the USA. It was only just in time. Outside of Alaska, numbers had crashed to about 400. Since then there has been a hotly argued programme of reintroduction. The most famous wolves in the United States live in the home of Yogi Bear – Yellowstone National Park.

The last native wolves in the Park area were killed between 1910 and 1926. But in a dramatic effort to turn back the clock, fourteen animals from Canada were released in the Park in 1995. They formed three

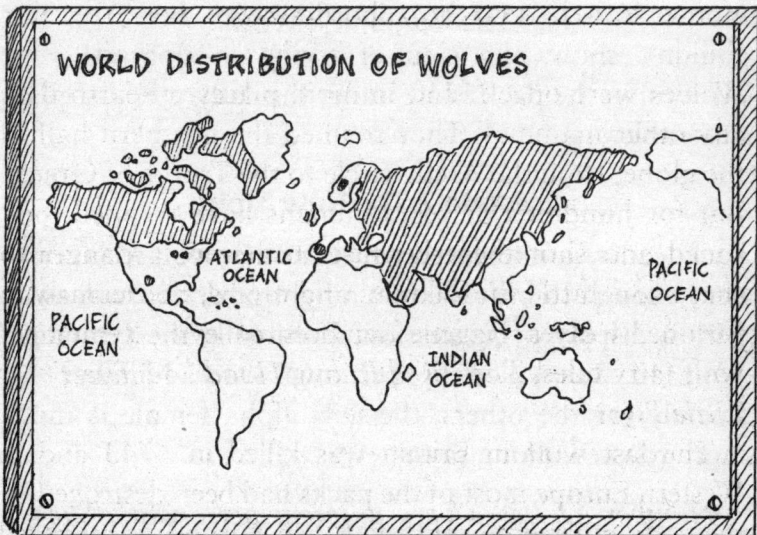

WORLD DISTRIBUTION OF WOLVES

ATLANTIC OCEAN

PACIFIC OCEAN

PACIFIC OCEAN

INDIAN OCEAN

packs and the population has gone from strength to strength ever since. By the winter of 2000 there were 120 adult wolves and around 60–70 new pups in Yellowstone and five wilderness areas nearby. Many of the wolves are tagged with radio collars, and biologists are keeping detailed records of their lives. Here's an episode from the Yellowstone wild-dog soap opera:

Episode 1: Murder Most Foul

The Druids Peak Pack was led by an alpha female called 'Wolf 40'. On 8 May 2000 she was found dying by a roadside in the Lamar valley region. Her body had several puncture wounds. Was it murder?

In a way, yes! Wolf 40 ruled her pack with an iron paw. Biologist Doug Smith commented: 'She was very aggressive. She was one of those drill sergeant-type moms. You had to be subordinate to her. You just couldn't show any sign of trying to upgrade your position in the pack.' Life under this lady was just plain miserable.

Episode 2: The New Alpha

Pack leaders are replaced when another wolf feels confident enough to beat them in a fight or drive them away with a display of aggression. Eventually the tyrannical Wolf 40 was killed by her own sister, Number 42. Luckily for the others, the new alpha female is much more relaxed. Doug says:

Number 42 has a very different personality. She's

tolerating a lot of behaviour that 40 wouldn't. She's not making the other females subordinate to her.

In a classic Hollywood happy ending the other females of the pack have adopted the young pups of the dead alpha – an act of kindness never recorded by wolf researchers before.

A Wider Recovery

The Yellowstone pattern is being repeated across the world. More than 3,500 wolves roam parts of eight US states, with thousands more in Alaska. In some areas numbers are so healthy that the American government has cut the legal protection given to wolves from 'endangered' to 'threatened'. This means that troublesome wolves that attack livestock can be shot by government agents. In France the last wolf was shot in 1927 but in the early 1990s new packs began to cross the mountains from Italy into the Mercantour National Park. In Russia intensive hunting, often from helicopters or planes, had cut the wolf population to 29,000 by 1988. Latest estimates claim numbers have recovered to at least 100,000.

The Scottish Wolf?

The Scottish Highlands cover an area of 25,000 square kilometres. This region is one of the best wilderness areas in Europe outside of Russia. In recent years there has been a programme of reintroducing species that were once native. This has worked well for birds – the red kite and the white-tailed sea eagle now soar the skies again. So what about mammals? A small population of beavers has already been brought back, but is there room for a large predator? The Wolf Specialist Group of the IUCN visited Scotland in 1994 and concluded that all the conditions are right for wolves to survive – not least because there are around 300,000 wild deer to prey on.

Will Scotland follow the American example – or will those ancient human fears keep the wolves away?

What Can You Do?

Maneaters are wild, magnificent and under extreme threat all over the planet. You want to help, but not enough to keep a tiger in your garage or a shark in your bath. So what else can you do? With a little thought you can be still part of their conservation.

Join Up

Join and support a conservation organization. Most rely on membership subscriptions and donations for their funds. They need your money and involvement. Read about their campaigns and see if there are any that are helping your favourite maneaters.

You can even adopt an animal. You pay £1–2 a month to help protect an animal in a threatened area and receive an adoption certificate and get regular progress reports.

Do something silly, or even something serious and responsible, to raise funds – walk around for an hour with jelly in your wellies or help an older person with the gardening.

Volunteer

Several organizations keep lists of where and when they want help. This might be anything from setting up nest tubes for dormice in Britain to erecting elephant-proof fences in Africa.

Campaign

If you feel strongly about an issue, like the threat to the Amazon rainforest from developments in Brazil – LET SOMEONE KNOW HOW YOU FEEL.

- Ask your teacher if you can hold a class or school assembly.
- Write to a national newspaper.
- Write to your MP at the House of Commons.
- Write to a foreign embassy.

You can find the addresses you need in your local library.

Recycle

Think about this rattling fact: every year the UK alone uses over 6 billion drinks cans.

Recycling means turning waste and rubbish like this

back into raw materials, so that they can be used again to make new items. So next time you are asked to take the old bottles to the bottle bank – don't argue. And don't stick the green glass in the brown glass container just because you are annoyed!

What's recycling got to do with maneaters? Remember, the biggest threat to most large predators is human misuse of their habitat – often to get at the natural resources like oil, minerals and timber, in wilderness areas. The more we can turn waste or rubbish back into raw materials, the better for the whole planet.

Be a Thoughtful Consumer

Go one step back from recycling. If you buy less you make less rubbish. Look for products that will last longer – don't be a fashion or logo victim. Buy fewer disposable items – choose your drinks in glass bottles rather than plastic, use a shopping bag rather than plastic carriers. If you are buying Christmas presents for the dog/Auntie Nelly's birthday choose gifts from a conservation group.

Be an Eco-Tourist

If you help decide where your family goes on holiday, adapt this sentence for your personal preferences:

'I don't want to go to Disneyland, let's go and see the polar bears in Canada/ lions in South Africa/ tigers in India instead. I hate Donald Duck, I want to ride the Tundra Buggy/ safari jeep.'

Now don't spoil it by breaking down and crying halfway through, say it as if you really mean it.

Seriously, eco-tourism can be a powerful conservation weapon. Tourist dollars are one of the best ways to stop poaching. Local people, who have to live with maneaters on their doorstep, can see that live animals are worth cash to them. It's a hard world and money talks.

Dig for Wildlife

Prepare for the ultimate sacrifice – next time Dad asks you for help in the garden reply: 'Certainly, honoured father, you will have my complete enthusiasm – if we go green in our horticultural habits.'

If you don't have a garden at home hijack a teacher to

plan a wildlife garden at school – he/she will have to agree that it's very educational.

Habitat is crucial for all wildlife – if you can't help a maneater directly you can set a good example. Even a small garden can be landscaped to attract birds, butterflies, insects and small animals. Choose your trees and shrubs carefully and you can have your own nature reserve.

Maneaters' Top Wildlife Websites

There are dozens of worthy organizations out there on the net. Have a browse – just type animal conservation into the search engines. These are some of my personal favourites:

www.seashepherd.org
Sea Shepherd International is an oceanic and conservation action force. They investigate and report 'pirates' who break laws and treaties protecting marine wildlife. This site is brilliantly designed and packed full of adventure. They don't back away from a fight!

Sea Shepherd has its own fleet, including the 6 ton *Mirage*, a two-person mini submarine built for the Norwegian Navy. In one campaign she was painted to resemble an orca whale to frighten other species away from an area where they would be in danger from human predators.

www.iucn.org
The World Conservation Union is the big player in international conservation. It was founded in 1948 and

operates in almost every country. Since 1963 the IUCN has compiled the *Red List of Threatened Species*. This is a massive inventory of the biodiversity of the planet and the risks that species face. There are eight doom-laden categories:

Extinct
Extinct in the Wild
Critically Endangered
Endangered
Vulnerable
Lower Risk
Data Deficient
Not Evaluated

The list includes planets and birds as well as animals – everything from moss to maneaters.

The Red List provides the scientific evidence to push governments into national and international action.

One arm of the IUCN is the Species Survival Commission. This is the network of volunteer scientists and conservation activists that does the research for the Red List. These volunteers are divided into dozens of specialist groups and many have their own websites. If you are a plant lover there's even a Cactus and Succulent Specialist Group. Two SGs make it on our hit list:

http://lynx.uio.no/catfolk
The Cat Specialist Group compiles data on all matters concerning wildcats. *Cat News*, their magazine, has lots

of big cat attack stories. The Species Accounts (that's descriptions of the cats) are very thorough – everything you need for a school project.

www.flmnh.ufl.edu/natsci/herptology/crocs/htm
The Crocodile Specialist Group has something to brag about: sixteen out of 23 species of crocodilians returned to abundance since 1971. How's this for a long boast:

> *This level of conservation success has not been achieved with primates, not with whales, not with spotted cats, not with parrots and macaws, nor with any other major wildlife group.*

Find out how it was done, what's happening in the croc world now and read the newsletter for up to date croc attack stories.

www.wwf.org
The World Wildlife Fund is one of the grandads of the conservation world. It has a punchy slogan: *Together, we can leave our children a living planet*. The website lets you visit the WWF global network to find out what's happening in countries as different as Poland, India and Cameroon.

www.5tigers.org
This site by the Tiger Information Centre provides information relevant to the preservation of the five surviving subspecies of tigers in the wild in Asia and in zoos worldwide. It's packed full of goodies, especially the up-to-date news.

www.igorilla.com/gorilla/animal/
Top Secret Animal Attack Files are opened to the public on this site. But it's a tongue in cheek claim because most of them come from newspaper reports sent in by respondents round the world. Good grisly fun.

www.wolfsociety.org.uk
The United Kingdom doesn't have any wild wolves – yet. But this site by the Wolf Society of Great Britain lets you know what the Brits are missing. It's particularly good on what is happening to European wolves. Save up and go on their wolf-spotting holidays to the Slovak mountains.

www.polarbearsalive.org
Polar Bears Alive is a cuddly site campaigning for *Ursus maritimus*.

Slogan: *For polar bear lovers all over the world.*

The organization was founded by the award-winning photographer Dan Guravich. Look out for his books in your local library – the pictures are stunning.

A selected list of titles available from Macmillan and Pan Books

---

Peter Hepplewhite and Neil Tonge

Animals in Danger	0 330 39338 3	£3.99
Animals to the Rescue	0 330 39337 5	£3.99

Philip Ardagh

WOW!

Events	0 330 48103 7	£2.99
Ideas	0 330 48101 0	£2.99
Discoveries	0 330 48100 2	£2.99
Inventions	0 330 48102 9	£2.99
